Understanding
Kanji Characters
by their Ancestral Forms

Learning **Kanji** *through pictures*

by

Ping-gam Go

Simplex Publications, San Francisco

By the same Author:
. *Read Chinese Today.*
. *What Character Is That? An Easy-Access Dictionary
of 5,000 Chinese Characters.*
. *Understanding Chinese Characters by their Ancestral Forms.*

Understanding Kanji Characters by their Ancestral Forms.
Copyright © 2000 **Gam P. Go.**

ISBN: 0-9623113-6-7

Printed in the U. S. A.

Contents

Introduction

There are two kinds of Kanji characters. Originally, Kanji characters were pictures or combination of pictures from which one derived their meanings

Lessons A and B contain such characters. They are called **"Pictograms "** (*picto* = picture; *gram* = writing). They were written with a stylus on bamboo or wood, or other suitable material. Only a thousand or two of them are known today.

A Chinese general who had to write a report at the end of each day, invented the writing brush. Writing with a brush using ink and paper was much easier and faster than writing with a stylus on bamboo or wood, etc.

However, the new method had its drawbacks. It led to alterations of the originals, deviating more and more from the original stylus writings, because the brush could not make the loops and intricate drawings that the original stylus written pictures contained.

Also, *because the brush could not make adequate drawings, new drawings were rarely created. Instead, a new character was formed consisting of two existing pictures. One picture showed to which group of characters the character belongs, and is called the "Radical "* (*radix* = root). *The other picture showed the (Chinese) pronunciation of the character, and is called the "Phonetic"* (*phone* = sound). This new kind of characters are known as **"Phonograms"** (*phone* = sound; *gram* = writing), as opposed to **"Pictograms"** above.

An example of a Phonogram 洋 Ocean [*Yang* [2]] consists of the *Radical* 氵 (Water), which tells us that the character belongs to the group of characters that *has something to do with "Water"*. And the *Phonetic* 羊 *Yang* [2] shows the (Chinese) pronunciation of the character.

With Pictograms we can derive the meaning of a character from the picture or combination of pictures contained in the character. This is not possible with Phonograms as we see above. We must simply memorize the meaning of a Phonogram!

v

This book contains 313 Kanji characters, which is about one-third of the required number of characters that an elementary school student in Japan should know. *

In order to learn above Kanji characters, we will study them in three different lessons:

Lesson A – Easy Kanji. In this lesson, we will study the *easy* cases. Their meanings can be easily derived from their ancestral forms.

Lesson B – Not So Easy Kanji. In this lesson, we will study the cases that are *not so easy to explain,* even though we know their ancestral forms.

Lesson C – Difficult Kanji. In this lesson, you will find the cases that are *difficult* to explain, namely the *Phonograms.*. There are no ancestral forms from which you can derive their meanings. You have to simply *memorize* their meanings.

---

* In Japan, 1, 006 Kanji characters are taught at the Elementary School.

Lesson
Easy Kanji

About half (40%) of all Kanji characters in this book can be learned easily, many of them very easily. There are 127 of such characters out of the total of 313 characters discussed in this book.

At the end of this Lesson, there is a **Review** section in which you can check your progress and determine which characters you know and which characters you do not know. You should study again the ones that you do not know.

Some characters are difficult, even though you know their ancestral forms. In those cases, you can follow the traditional method, namely by *writing down those characters several times in a row, while pronouncing their meanings.* A chapter **"How to Write a Kanji Character"** appears in the **Appendix**.

The most simple Kanji characters are found in the Group NUMBERS . They are the characters for the numbers ONE 一, TWO 二 and THREE 三 , namely 一 *(one stroke)*, 二 *(two strokes)* and 三 *(three strokes)*.

FOUR 四 was originally written 𝍶 *(a quantity ○ that can be divided 八 into two equal portions)*. SIX 六 is another equal number; it was written 𝍶 , *with a dot •* *to distinguish it from FOUR*. How about EIGHT 八? That is another equal number ! Well, it was written 八 , which means *a quantity consisting of two equal halves:* ノ *and* 乚.

FIVE 五 was considered a *unit* because we have on each of our hands "five" fingers. It is still used as a unit in the abacus, the old counting instrument The ancient writing for "five" is 𝕏 .

SEVEN 七 was also considered a *unit.* It was namely a unit in fortune-telling. It was written as a unit with a "tail" 𠃉 , to distinguish it from the unit "ten" 十 .

TEN 十 , we all know, is a *unit* in counting and written as a symmetric "cross", the same as in the ancient writing 十 .

NINE 九 , being almost the unit "ten" 九 , was written as *"a wavy ten"* .

The character for MANY 多 is represented by *two objects.* Here "object" is represented by the symbol for MOUTH ▽ , a very simple symbol and easy to write.

A FEW, or A LITTLE 少 is *what is left after a portion is taken away* 彡 *from something what is already SMALL* 小 *(an object 八 split 丨 into two parts* ノ *and* 丶 *):* 少.

A3

In the Group **HUMAN BODY** we find other characters that are very easy to understand once you see their original stylus writings. The **MOUTH** 口 was originally written ⊌ .
The **TONGUE** 舌 was a picture of the *"tongue"* ⍦ *coming out from the "mouth"* ⊌ and written ⍦.

The **EYE** 目 was formerly written ⬭ and *later written vertically ⊖ in order to save writing space.* The **EAR** 耳 was written ⌾ . The **HAND** 手 was a picture of the *hand which clearly shows the five fingers* ⍦ . And **HAIR** 毛 was a *clear picture of a bundle of hair* ⍦ .

HEART now written in Kanji 心 was formerly an appropriate picture of the heart ⍦ showing *the "open sac"* ⍦, *the "lobes"* ⍦ , and the "aorta" ⌐ .

The Group **PERSONS** contains several Kanji characters that are also easy to understand by knowing their original writings. The character for **PERSON** (a human being) 人 , originally written ⍦ represents *the two "legs" of a person,* an appropriate symbol because a person as a rule is standing on his or her legs.

A **CHILD** in Kanji is 子. It was originally written ⍦ : *a newborn baby with the legs still bound in swathes.*

A **WOMAN** 女 was before written ⍦ , i.e. *a woman with a curvy figure,* a simple and very effective symbol. By adding two short strokes, we get ⍦ , which is *a woman with prominent breasts, namely a "mother", because in the old days a mother gave breast-feeding to her child.* When written in Kanji, **MOTHER** is 母 .

The Kanji for **FATHER** 父 is not difficult to understand if you know it is is *a hand* ∋ *holding a rod* / *expressing authority:* ⳗ .

Two hands working in the same direction ⻖ was an appropriate symbol for **FRIEND**, which in Kanji is 友 .

The character for **KING** 王 was a simple symbol 王 , which means the *mediator* | *between Heaven* ⁻ , *Earth and Man* ⁻ . **EMPRESS** 后 or 后 as written with the stylus, means *a person* ⼏ (see MAN) *who is bending over* ⼾ *to shout* ⼞ (MOUTH) *orders to her subjects.*

In the Group | **ANIMALS** | we find some easy-to-remember animals. The Kanji character for **BIRD** 鳥 is easy to remember, if we know that the original writing was 鳥 . The same with **FISH** 魚 the original writing of which was 魚 .

The character for **OX**, or **COW** or **CATTLE** is 牛 . We can remember that character by looking at its original stylus-written symbol 牛 . It is *an ox seen from behind.* The top part 屮 represents "the head with the horns", which is superimposed on ⼀ , which represents "the two hind legs and tail".

The brush-written Kanji for **DOG** is 犬 . The original stylus-written symbol was 犬 , which is *a picture of a dog seen from the front.* You see "the body with the two front legs " ⼏ and "the head (turned aside)" ⼂ .

The character for **SHEEP** is 羊 , which was originally written 羊. It is *a sheep seen from behind.* You can see the "horns" written as ⋎ , superimposed on ⼲, representing "the four feet and tail" seen from behind.

And finally, everybody will recognize this elegant symbol as that for a **HORSE** 駡 . The modern character is awkward, namely 馬 .

Many Kanji characters in the Group │ **VEGETATION** │ can be easily recognized and remembered. The Kanji word for **TREE** is 木 . The original writing is basicly the same, namely 朱 , showing the *trunk* │ the *branches* ∪ and the *roots* ∧ . When a "dash" is added at the bottom under the "roots" 本 , the character means **ROOT, ORIGIN,** or also **BOOK.** The symbol 果 , in Kanji 果 , means **FRUIT.** It shows *a fruit* ⊕ *growing on a tree* 朱 . The fruit **MELON** 瓜 is a *picture of a melon plant and its fruit* 瓜 .

Two "trees" put next to each other 林 means *many trees,* representing a **FOREST, WOOD** or **GROVE,** which is in Kanji 林 .

BAMBOO 竹 is represented by *trees with drooping leaves* 竹 .

A series of characters in the Group │ **NATURE** │ can also be easily understood; we only have to see their ancient stylus-written forms. For example, the Kanji character for **SUN** 日 was *a circle with a "dash" inside* ⊝ . And **MOON** 月 was *a picture of a crescent moon* 🌙 . **HEAVEN** 天 was written as 天 , which means *that which expands* ⌐ *over mankind* 大 (see BIG). And the **EARTH** 土 was written as *the layer* = *from which all things came out* ¡ : 土 . **MOUNTAIN** 山 was *a picture of a mountain* Ѱ . **RIVER** 川 was a *big stream that consists of smaller streams* ⦀ . **WATER** 水 itself was *a stream* ⟍ *in which whirls of water* ⦙ : ⫶ .

A6

FIRE 火 was written as *a pile of wood burning with flames* 灬 .

ICE 氷 being *WATER* 川 *that has crystallized and* 人 *being the crystals,* was written as 冰 . RAIN 雨 being *drops of water* == *falling down* | *from the clouds* ⌒ *suspended from the sky* —, was written as 雨 .

ISLAND 島 was written 島 , because it can be regarded a *MOUNTAIN* 山 *in the sea on which BIRDs* 鳥 *can rest while crossing the sea.* GOLD 金 was written as 金 , which shows *four nuggets* 兰 *burried (* ⌒ *covered) in the ground* (*EARTH* 土).

The Group COLORS contains several Kanji characters that are easy to know and remember. For example, the character **WHITE** 白 was represented by *the SUN* ☉ *just rising above the horizon and causing the sky to become "white";* 白.
BLACK 黒 is *the color of soot* ⅲ *deposited by a smoky FIRE* 炎 *around a vent* ⊕ : 黑 . And **YELLOW** 黄 is *the fiery glow* 𢦏 *(a MAN* 人 *carrying a torch* 𠂤 *) from the fields* ⊕ *at harvest time:* 黄 .

Some important Kanji characters in the group FOOD are easy to remember. They are first of all **RICE** 米 , which formerly written as 米 shows *four grains of rice scattered* 米 *due to thrashing* ┼ . **MEAT** 肉 *were strips of dried meat bundled together* 肉 . **FOOD** 食 in general, or **TO EAT** was represented by a *pot with contents* ☺ *a ladle* ∠ *and the symbol* △ *(three lines coming together) to suggest mixing:* 食 . And **WINE** 酒 was a WINE JUG 酉 and its liquid ⅲ (see WATER) contents: 酒 .

The Kanji for **KNIFE** 刀 was originally written ⼑ . It is *a simple picture of a knife; later the handle was curved upwards to save writing space* ⼑ . Another character in the Group OBJECTS is **ARROW** 矢 , which was formerly written 矢. And the Kanji for **TREASURE** 宝 was 玉 *a priceless piece of JADE [the gem • that only kings* 王 *(the mediator | between Heaven* ‾ *, Earth* _ *, and Man* — *) could possess] kept in one's house* ⼏ *(DWELLING):* 宝 . You can also remember the Kanji for **CART** 車 if you know that the ancient writing was *a cart seen from above*, namely 車 . It shows the *body* ⊕ , *axle* | and ⼆ *wheels* .

In the Group ENTERPRISE , the word **WORK** is written 工 in Kanji. The ancient writing was basicly the same, namely 工. It represents *the ancient carpenter's square* (a tool to test right angles), used as a symbol for "work". **TO BUY** 買 was written 買 . It means *to put something of value* (represented by SHELL 貝 , formerly used as money) *into a shopping net* ⼍, *after it has been "bought"*. **TO SELL** 売 was the same symbol as "to buy", but with on top the symbol 士 (new shoots ⼃ coming out from the mother-plant ⼃): 賣 . It means *to take out something of value from a shopping net in order to "sell" it.*

PROFIT 利 was written 利 , which means: *the GRAIN* 禾 *has been cut* ⼑ *(KNIFE) and will soon yield profit.* **TRADE** 貿 had a very appropriate symbol, namely 貿 . It represents *a DOOR* 門 *that is open* 卯 *and money (* 貝 SHELL, formerly used as money) *passing through it.*

刀

矢

宝

車

工

買

売

利

貿

In the Group INSTITUTIONS we find several characters that we can learn and easily remember. The word MARKET, in Kanji 市 , was formerly written as 㞑 . It represents *an open space ノ⌒ grown with grass 屮 where one obtains ᒎ one's necessities.* And CAPITAL or METROPOLIS 京 is *a picture of the capital's tower* 京 . GOVERNMENT 官 is represented by the "*Capitol*", building 宀 (see DWELLING) *with many steps* 㠯 : 官 . STREET 街 is represented by *footsteps* 彳 (see GO) *and a part of the land* 圭 [土 EARTH (2x)] *on which people walk* 街 .

EVENING 夕 is represented by *a wavy half-moon , just appearing above the horizon:* ㇞ . Another word in the Group TIME is NOON 午 which is *a picture of an ancient sun-dial to mark the noon-time:* 夲 . And MORNING 早 is *when the SUN* ⊖ *has just risen to the height of a soldier's helmet* 甲 : 昻 . NIGHT 夜 is *when a person* 大 (see BIG) *is turning aside* ノ *in order to sleep, late in the EVENING* 夕 : 夜 . MOON or MONTH 月 is *a picture of a crescent moon* 月 .

The WINTER 冬 formerly written as 夅 is *the end* 夊 (*the knot at the end of a sewing thread*) *of the year when ice* 冫 (*ice crystals*) *appear.* And SPRING 春 formerly 萅 , *a picture of the SUN* ⊖ *and the sprouting of plants* 屮屮 (ψψ*plants*). Formerly SUMMER 夏 was pictured as *a person [represented by the nose* 自 (see NOSE) *] with idle hands* ㇇ *walking at leisure* 夊 (*see PURSUE*): 夏 .

In the Group | **LOCATIONS** | , you will find Kanji characters that you can easily remember after you have seen their original stylus-written forms. For example, the two characters **TOP** 上 and **BOTTOM** 下 were originally very simple symbols, namely ⊥ and ⊤ . They mean: *an object │ above a certain level ＿* and *an object │ below a certain level ─* . The word **INSIDE** 内 was written 内, which means: *to ENTER 人 inside a certain space ∩* . **MIDDLE** 中 was written 〵├┤, meaning *a target ├┤ pierced │ in the center by an arrow* .

LEFT 左 was *the "left hand"* : *the one that holds the carpenter's square* 工 : . And **RIGHT** 右 was *the "right hand"* : *the one that we use when we eat (* ⊔ *MOUTH):* .

NORTH 北, *formerly* 〵〳 : *two persons* 〳〳 *(see MAN) turning their backs to the North . (Formerly facing the South was a custom during ceremonies; the Chinese Emperor faced the South to look over his domain.)* **SOUTH** 南, *formerly the area ⟨ ⟨ where vegetation (plant) expands continuously (see PESTLE , with additional stroke -- to suggest continuity).* **EAST** 東 , *formerly : the SUN ⊙ is in the East when it is so low that one can see it behind the trees 木 (of the Eastern mountains).* **WEST** 西 , *formerly : when the birds sit on their nests , it is evening and the sun is in the West.*

In the Group **BUILDINGS** , the word for **DOOR** or
GATE is in Kanji 門 . The ancient writing is 門 , which
is very easy to remember, because it is *a simple picture of
a 'saloon-door' with two swinging half-doors.* The Kanji
for **ROOM** is 室, formerly 室 . It represents *a place in
the house* 宀 *(DWELLING) to which one returns after
work (* 𠃊 *bird with wings backwards, coming down to
EARTH* 土 *).* **HOME** or **HOUSE(HOLD)** 家 , formerly
家 means *a DWELLING* 宀 *where PIGS* 豕 *have free
entry. (To make sure that they were adequately fed, pigs
had the same privileges as dogs today.)* The word for
HALL or **TEMPLE** 堂 is basicly the same as the ancient
writing 堂 . It is *a building (* 宀 *DWELLING) with a
crest* 小 *and window* ○ *, where soil* 土 *(EARTH) is shel-
tered.* And **PALACE** 宮 is also easy to remember, because the ancient writing 宮 means *a DWELLING* 宀
which contains a series of rooms 呂 *.*

Several words relating to **TRAVEL** are not difficult
to remember once you see the ancient forms. They are
GO OUT 出 formerly written 出 . It represents *new
shoots* 屮 *that come out from the mother-plant* 凵 *.*
ARRIVE (AT) 至 was written before as 至 . *It means
a bird with wings backwards* 𠃊 *coming down to the EARTH*
土 *.* **BOAT** 舟 was written 舟 , which represents *a
hollowed tree trunk (* 片 *is half of a TREE* 木 *) which
stands for a boat.* **SHIP** 船, formerly 船 is *a BOAT*

that cleaves 八 *the surface* 彐 *of the water.* **FLY** 飛 is easy to remember, because the ancient writing was that of *a flying crane* 𠇍 .

Under GOOD LUCK SIGNS there are some characters that are easy to remember. The word for **JOY** is in Kanji 喜 . The ancestral form represents *"music" (a HAND* 彐 *holding a stick* ⊤ *that beats a drum-on-a-stand* 豆 *) and "singing"* ▽ *(MOUTH)*: 𠱷 . **MUSIC** is 楽 written in Kanji. The ancient writing 樂 explains why it is so, because it is *a picture of a musical instrument, namely a frame with a "drum" (in the middle) and "bells" (on the side).*

There are many words in the Group ADJECTIVES that you can easily remember. First of all, **SWEET** 甘 was pictured as *something* ⁓ *that is "sweet" being held in our MOUTH* ▽: 甘 . **PEACEFUL** 安 is *when a WOMAN* 女 *is inside the house* 宀 *(see DWELLING)*: 安 . **COMPLETE** 全 is *when our WORK* 工 *is completed* *(three lines joined together* △ *)*: 全 . **GOOD** 好 is *when* *a man has a wife* 女 *(WOMAN) and children* 子 *(CHILD)*: 女子 . **STRAIGHT** 直 is *when TEN* + *EYEs* 目 *are look-* *ing at something and finding nothing is wrong (* ∟ *straight angle)*: 直 . **BRIGHT** 明 is *when the MOON* 月 *is shin-* *ing through the window* 囧 *and the room is "brightly" lit*: 明 . **BEAUTIFUL** 美 is *when something is as beautiful*

as a big sheep (大 *BIG*; 羊 *SHEEP*) *with fully developed*
horns : 美. **WEAK** 弱 is represented by *the fluffy feathers*
of a young and 'weak' bird: 弱 . And **PRECIOUS** 貴 is
a basket 产 *filled with money* (貝 *SHELL, formerly used*
as money in ancient China): 貴 .

There are four very common Kanji characters in Group
SIZE that you can remember easily. The word for **BIG**
or **GREAT** in Kanji is 大 . It is represented by *a MAN with*
outstretched arms 大 *as if showing how big the fish was that*
he caught lately. Another MAN with arms alongside his
body 小 *as if to show how small the fish was that he caught*
that day, represents the word **SMALL** 小. (Other expla-
tion for SMALL: *an object* 八 *that is split* | *into two:* 小.)
HIGH 高 is represented by a picture of a tower: 高.

The Group VERBS has also a number of Kanji words
easy to remember. All you have to do is to look at their
original writings. For example, two words that you often
see on a door are: **PUSH** 押 and **PULL** 引 . *A HAND*
and a symbol 甲 *representing a downward motion* (| *going*
down from 田 *)*. 押, means "push". And *to pull* | *at the*
string of a bow 弓 :引 , means "pull". **ENTER** 入 is
basicly the same writing, namely 人 , and represents *a plant*
with its roots penetrating the soil. **STAND** 立 is a person
(see BIG) standing on the ground: 立 . **TURN** 回 is *a*
whirlpool in which the water turns around rapidly: 回 .

A13

The word for **SAY** is in Kanji and is represented by *the words (⸗ sound waves) that are produced by the TONGUE* 🙶 : 🙷 . **SEE** 見 is pictured by *the EYE* ⊖ *of a person (a being standing on two legs* 儿 *):* 見 . Another word for **SEE** or **WATCH** 看 was written as 看 , which *is a HAND* 手 *shading the EYE* ⊖ *in order to see better.*

COME 来 was 來 and is *a person* 大 *(see BIG) coming down the road with ears of corn* ⋀⋀ *over his shoulders.*

ASK 問 is *to be at the DOOR* 門 *before leaving and asking (* ⊓ *MOUTH) another person a question* 問 .

OPEN (v) 開 is *a pair of HANDs* 廾 *removing the bar* — *from the DOOR* 門 : 開 . **CLOSE** or **SHUT** 閉 is *when the bars* 丰 *are behind the DOOR* 門 : 閉 .

Under **MISCELLANEOUS** there are two characters that are very simple and easy to remember. The word for **RICE FIELD** 田 was the same, namely ⊕ . **NOT** 不 is represented by an upward flying bird with wings backwards 不 who tries in vain to reach the sky 不 .

Review Lesson A

After you have carefully studied Lesson A, you should review it. It does take time and patience to know all characters.

As a first step, take | **Review No.1** | (p. A17) and *hi-lite* (or *circle*) all characters that you know. This allows you to see the characters that you *do not* know. You now go back to study again those unknown characters.

After a day or two, you take| **Review No. 2** |and follow the same procedure. You should now know more characters than the first time.

After doing | **Review No. 3** |and| **Review No. 4** |, you should know all characters of Lesson A.

Warning - avoid getting fines! If this book is a book from the Library, *do not hi-lite or circle in this book!* Make first copies of the pages that you need and hi-lite or circle there!

A								
一[1]	二[2]	三[3]	四[4]	五[5]	六[6]	七[7]	八[8]	九[9]
十[10]	多[11]	少[12]	**B** 口[1]	舌[2]	目[3]	耳[4]	手[5]	毛[6]
心[7]	人[8]	子[9]	女[10]	母[11]	**C** 父[1]	友[2]	王[3]	后[4]
D 馬[1]	木[2]	本[3]	果[4]	鳥[5]	魚[6]	牛[7]	犬[8]	羊[9]
瓜[5]	林[6]	竹[7]	日[8]	月[9]	天[10]	土[11]	山[12]	川[13]
水[14]	**E** 火[1]	氷[2]	雨[3]	島[4]	金[5]	白[6]	黒[7]	黄[8]
米[9]	肉[10]	食[11]	酒[12]	**F** 刀[1]	矢[2]	玉[3]	車[4]	工[5]
G 市[1]	京[2]	官[3]	街[4]	夕[5]	買[6]	売[7]	利[8]	貿[9]
午[6]	早[7]	夜[8]	月[9]	冬[10]	春[11]	夏[12]	**H** 上[1]	下[2]
I 門[1]	内[3]	中[4]	左[5]	右[6]	北[7]	南[8]	東[9]	西[10]
室[2]	家[3]	堂[4]	宮[5]	出[6]	至[7]	舟[8]	船[9]	**J** 飛[1]
喜[2]	楽[3]	甘[4]	安[5]	全[6]	好[7]	直[8]	明[9]	美[10]
K 弱[1]	貴[2]	大[3]	小[4]	高[5]	押[6]	引[7]	入[8]	立[9]
L 言[1]	見[2]	看[3]	来[4]	問[5]	開[6]	閉[7]	田[8]	回[10]
不[9]								

LIST OF EASY CHARACTERS
Please, hi-lite the ones that you know already. *If this book is a Library Book, please, make a copy first !*

REVIEW No. 1

A 一[1]	二[2]	三[3]	四[4]	五[5]	六[6]	七[7]	八[8]	九[9]
十[10]	多[11]	少[12]	B 口[1]	舌[2]	目[3]	耳[4]	手[5]	毛[6]
心[7]	人[8]	子[9]	女[10]	母[11]	C 父[1]	友[2]	王[3]	后[4]
D 馬[1]	木[2]	本[3]	果[4]	鳥[5]	魚[6]	牛[7]	犬[8]	羊[9]
瓜[5]	林[6]	竹[7]	日[8]	月[9]	天[10]	土[11]	山[12]	川[13]
水[14]	E 火[1]	氷[2]	雨[3]	島[4]	金[5]	白[6]	黒[7]	黄[8]
米[9]	肉[10]	食[11]	酒[12]	F 刀[1]	矢[2]	玉[3]	車[4]	工[5]
G 帀[1]	京[2]	官[3]	街[4]	夕[5]	買[6]	売[7]	利[8]	貿[9]
午[6]	早[7]	夜[8]	月[9]	冬[10]	春[11]	夏[12]	H 上[1]	下[2]
I 門[1]	内[3]	中[4]	左[5]	右[6]	北[7]	南[8]	東[9]	西[10]
室[2]	家[3]	堂[4]	宮[5]	出[6]	至[7]	舟[8]	船[9]	J 飛[1]
喜[2]	楽[3]	甘[4]	安[5]	全[6]	好[7]	直[8]	明[9]	美[10]
K 弱[1]	貴[2]	大[3]	小[4]	高[5]	押[6]	引[7]	入[8]	立[9]
L 言[1]	見[2]	看[3]	来[4]	問[5]	開[6]	閉[7]	田[8]	回[10]
不[9]								

LIST OF EASY CHARACTERS
Please, hi-lite the ones that you know already. *If this book is a Library Book, please, make a copy first !*

A18

A1 一	2 二	3 三	4 四	5 五	6 六	7 七	8 八	9 九
10 十	11 多	12 少	**B**1 口	2 舌	3 目	4 耳	5 手	6 毛
7 心	8 人	9 子	10 女	11 母	**C**1 父	2 友	3 王	4 后
D1 馬	2 木	3 本	4 果	5 鳥	6 魚	7 牛	8 犬	9 羊
5 瓜	6 林	7 竹	8 日	9 月	10 天	11 土	12 山	13 川
14 水	**E**1 火	2 氷	3 雨	4 島	5 金	6 白	7 黒	8 黄
9 米	10 肉	11 食	12 酒	**F**1 刀	2 矢	3 玉	4 車	5 工
G1 市	2 京	3 官	4 街	5 夕	6 買	7 売	8 利	9 貿
6 午	7 早	8 夜	9 月	10 冬	11 春	12 夏	**H**1 上	2 下
I1 門	3 内	4 中	5 左	6 右	7 北	8 南	9 東	10 西
2 室	3 家	4 堂	5 宮	6 出	7 至	8 舟	9 船	**J**1 飛
2 喜	3 楽	4 甘	5 安	6 全	7 好	8 直	9 明	10 美
K1 弱	2 貴	3 大	4 小	5 高	6 押	7 引	8 入	9 立
L1 言	2 見	3 看	4 来	5 問	6 開	7 閉	8 田	10 回
9 不								

LIST OF EASY CHARACTERS

Please, hi-lite the ones that you know already. *If this book is a Library Book, please, make a copy first !*

A19

A 一¹	二²	三³	四⁴	五⁵	六⁶	七⁷	八⁸	九⁹
十¹⁰	多¹¹	少¹²	**B** 口¹	舌²	目³	耳⁴	手⁵	毛⁶
心⁷	人⁸	子⁹	女¹⁰	母¹¹	**C** 父¹	友²	王³	后⁴
D 馬¹	木²	本³	果⁴	鳥⁵	魚⁶	牛⁷	犬⁸	羊⁹
瓜⁵	林⁶	竹⁷	日⁸	月⁹	天¹⁰	土¹¹	山¹²	川¹³
水¹⁴	**E** 火¹	氷²	雨³	島⁴	金⁵	白⁶	黒⁷	黄⁸
米⁹	肉¹⁰	食¹¹	酒¹²	**F** 刀¹	矢²	玉³	車⁴	工⁵
G 市¹	京²	官³	街⁴	夕⁵	買⁶	売⁷	利⁸	貿⁹
午⁶	早⁷	夜⁸	月⁹	冬¹⁰	春¹¹	夏¹²	**H** 上¹	下²
I 門¹	内³	中⁴	左⁵	右⁶	北⁷	南⁸	東⁹	西¹⁰
室²	家³	堂⁴	宮⁵	出⁶	至⁷	舟⁸	船⁹	**J** 飛¹
喜²	楽³	甘⁴	安⁵	全⁶	好⁷	直⁸	明⁹	美¹⁰
K 弱¹	貴²	大³	小⁴	高⁵	押⁶	引⁷	入⁸	立⁹
L 言¹	見²	看³	来⁴	問⁵	開⁶	閉⁷	田⁸	回¹⁰
不⁹								

LIST OF EASY CHARACTERS

Please, hi-lite the ones that you know already. *If this book is a Library Book, please, make a copy first!*

REVIEW No. 4

Lesson B
Not So Easy Kanji

Another half (40%) or 141 characters out of the total of 313 characters in this book are *not so easy to learn*, even though in this lesson (pp. B3-B29) they are adequately explained through their ancestral forms. Often you have to use a great deal of your imagination in order to understand them.

We will discuss the characters in Groups, alphabetically as is also done in the Dictionary. The characters are accompanied by Character Numbers as given to them in the Dictionary, to allow you to find them there. The Dictionary contains all information about the characters: their pronunciation(s), their meaning(s).

After you have finished studying Lesson B, please, review all characters of that lesson using ⟨ **Review I** ⟩, on pages B31-B34. In Review I the characters are shown *with their ancestral forms* to help you remember their meanings.

After you have done Review I , you should go to ⟨ **Review II** ⟩ , on pages B35-B43 which lists the characters *without their ancestral forms.*

Some characters are difficult, even though you know their ancestral forms. In those cases, you can follow the traditional method, namely by *writing down those characters several times in a row, while pronouncing meanings.* A chapter **"How to Write a Kanji Character"** appears in the **Appendix**.

1 Starting with the Group | **ADJECTIVES** |, the first Kanji we encounter is **ROUND** 丸, which is represented by *a person* 丿 *(see MAN) who is rolling down a CLIFF* 丶: 丸.

7 The adjective **AGED** 老 is pictured by *hair* 耂 *that has changed (a person* 丿 *(see MAN) who has changed his position* 匕 *- is upside down) and become white:* 耂.

10 **GOOD** 良 is *a gift* ⊖ *coming down* ⼕ *from Heaven that is so good that we can not refuse to accept it (stop* ⼂ *in its fall* 人 *):* 良.

14 The word **CLEAR** 亮 can be pictured as a *person* 人 *(MAN) who has a 'clear' mind, i.e. as a person who lives in a big city* 亯 *(capital – picture of the capital's tower) and is more enlightened than one living outside:* 亮.

15 **YOUNG** 若 can be represented by *young herbs (* 艸 *GRASS) that are gathered (* 彐 *HAND) in order to be consumed (* 口 *MOUTH):* 若.

17 And **STRONG** 強 is like *a beetle* 虫 *(see INSECT) that can bounce (* 弓 *BOW) up in the air and falls on its back* 厶 *:* 強.

18 **BAD** 悪 is represented by *a HEART* 心 *that is evil (the symbol for WORK* 工 *that is deformed* 亞 *):* 悪.

20 **COLD** 寒 is pictured by *a person* 个 *(MAN) who is nestled inside* 宀 *(DWELLING) straw* 茻 *, as a protection against the freezing* 冫 *(ICE) weather:* 寒.

21 And **NEW** 新 is *to cut (* 斤 *AXE) new branches from a TREE* 木 *, which were used to beat (* 辛 *OFFEND) criminals):* 新.

22 ALONE 寡 are *persons* 頁 *(HEAD) who used to live in the same house* 宀 *(DWELLING) and now separated* 八 (刀 *KNIFE) from each other:*  .

23 The word for BEAUTIFUL 麗 *is represented by a pair of beautiful earrings* ББ *and a DEER* 鹿 *with beautiful antlers* ΨΨ : .

NOTE: **ADJECTIVES** has 23 characters (Dict. pp. 1-3).
There are 3 Phonograms (Dict. pp. 1-3).
There are 9 Easy Characters (**Lesson A**, pp. A12-13).
There are 11 Not So Easy characters (above).

Do you still know the meanings of the Easy Characters mentioned above and printed here?
Please, go to **Lesson A** pp. A12-13 if you
do not know all of them!

好	甘	弱
直	安	貴
明	全	
美		

Attention, please!
For Phonograms see **Lesson C** – Difficult characters.

26   The next Group we will discuss is the Group ANIMALS .
The Kanji for **INSECT** 虫 was originally *a picture of a worm,*
and written as 〢 .

28 **SHELL** 貝 , originally 貝 is a picture of a 'cowrie', a small
seashell, formerly used as money in certain parts of Asia.

29   The original writing for **TIGER** 虎 was 虎 , which represents the *stripes of a tiger.* *

31   The Kanji character for **DRAGON** 竜 is not so easy to explain. The current writing is a simplified form of 龍 .   The
stylus writing was 龍 . It represents *a dragon* 竜 *, which was
flying (𦐂 wings) to the sky* = . [*It was formerly believed that
a dragon flew to the sky and thereby caused rain, after it was
sitting in the well during the dry season.*]

33   The original writing for **PIG** 豚 consists of two symbols
肉 *(FLESH)* and 豕 *(PIG).* It means *PIG, the FLESH of
which is normally consumed:* 肉豕 .

35   **DEER** 鹿 was originally written 鹿 , consisting of the
body ⊐ , the *head* ⊬ , the *antlers* ψ , and the *feet* 𠃊
of the animal.

36   And **BEAR** 熊 was originally written 熊 , consisting of
the *body* 肉 *(FLESH),* the *head* 呂 , the *claws* 𠃊 , and the
feet 灬 of the animal.

* The symbol 儿 represents the two legs of a human being (see
MAN), because a Tiger can stand up like a human being.

No.37 鶏 **CHICKEN** is a *Phonogram* and will be
put under **Lesson C** ("Difficult Characters").

B5

38   The next Group we will discuss is | **BUILDINGS** |. The Kanji for **DOOR** 戸 , formerly ⼾ , is a picture of the *left-hand leaf of a swinging door* 門 .

42   **HOUSE** 屋 , originally  is *a place where a person* 尸 *(see CORPSE) can always retreat* 至 *(a bird ⽧ with its wings backward, which is coming down to EARTH* ⼟ *):  .*

NOTE: **BUILDINGS** has 12 characters (Dict. pp. 6-7).
        There are 5 Phonograms (Dict. pp. 6-7).
        There are 5 Easy Characters (**Lesson A**, p. A11).
        There are 2 Not So Easy characters (above).

       Do you still know the mean-
         ings of the Easy Characters men-
tioned above and printed here?
Please, go to **Lesson A** p. A11 if you
do not know all of them!

門 室
家 堂
宮

NOTE: **ANIMALS** has 14 characters (Dict. pp. 4-5).
        There is 1 Phonogram (Dict. pp. 4- 5).
        There are 6 Easy Characters (**Lesson A**, pp. A5-6).
        There are 7 Not So Easy characters (above).

       Do you still know the mean-
         ings of the Easy Characters men-
tioned above and printed here?
Please, go to **Lesson A** pp. A5-6 if you
do not know all of them!

鳥 犬
魚 羊
牛 馬

Attention, please!
For Phonograms see **Lesson C** – Difficult characters.

51   We come now to the Group | **COLORS** | . The Kanji 色
for **COLOR** was represented by *a person* ⟨ *(see MAN) who
has a red (color of a SEAL* ㄗ *) face:* 咼 .

52   **RED** 赤 is pictured by *an angry person* 大 *(see BIG) whose
face has turned red (* 火 *FIRE):* 赤 .

53   **BLUE** and **GREEN** 青 , are both represented by *the color (a
substance* • *in a crucible* 凵 *which is 'colored' by heat) of a
young plant* 屮 *that is emerging from the EARTH* 土 : 青 .

NOTE: **COLORS** has 7 characters (Dict. p. 8).
       There is 1 Phonogram (Dict. p. 8).
       There are 3 Easy Characters (**Lesson A**, p. A7).
       There are 3 Not So Easy characters (above).

      Do you still know the mean-
        ings of the Easy Characters men-
tioned above and printed here?
Please, go to **Lesson A** p. A7 if you
do not know all of them!

白

黒

黄

Attention, please!
For Phonograms see **Lesson C** - Difficult characters.

We will now discuss Group | ENTERPRISE | . The Kanji

59 司 means CONTROL(v). It is represented by *a picture of a person* 人 *(MAN) who is bending over* ヲ *in order to shout* (凵 *MOUTH) his or her orders:* 司 .

60 The word for ADD (v) 加 is *STRENGTH* 力 *"added" to one's speech* (凵 *MOUTH):* 加 .

64 TRADE is 商 written in Kanji. The original writing was 商 , which means that it is *an enterprise that is created when WORDS* 言 *are spoken inside* 内 *(an object ENTERing* 人 *a certain space* ⊓ *) a room, lasting several days* (☉☉ *SUNs)*.

68 BUSINESS, INDUSTRY 業 *was pictured as a TREE* 木 *that is crowned with its foliage* 丵 *symbolizing a person's activity and its results:* 業 .

NOTE: ENTERPRISE has 12 characters (Dict. pp. 9-10).
　　　There are 3 Phonograms (Dict. pp. 9-10).
　　　There are 5 Easy Characters (**Lesson A**, p. A8).
　　　There are 4 Not So Easy characters (above).

Do you still know the meanings of the Easy Characters mentioned above and printed here?
Please, go to **Lesson A** p. A8 if you do not know all of them!

Attention, please!
For Phonograms see **Lesson C** – Difficult characters.

B8

71   The next Group is **FOOD** . The Kanji 卵 means **EGG**. The original writing was 戼 , representing *the female ovaries and oviduct*.

72   TEA is in Kanji 茶 The stylus writing was 茶 . It means *the tree-like (木 TREE) plant* ψψ *(GRASS) that gives joy (joyful drink) to mankind (ᕧ see MAN).*

NOTE: **FOOD** has 7 characters (Dict. p. 11).
There is 1 Phonogram (Dict. p. 11).
There are 4 Easy Characters (**Lesson A**, p. A7).
There are 2 Not So Easy characters (above).

Do you still know the meanings of the Easy Characters mentioned above and printed here?
Please, go to **Lesson A** p. A7 if you do not know all of them!

米 肉
酒 食

Attention, please!
For Phonograms see **Lesson C** – Difficult characters.

We will come now to the Group | **GOOD LUCK SIGNS** |

76   EVEN 平 was originally written 平̄, representing *the breath ɔ that is going through an obstacle -- and spreading out evenly* π .

77   GOOD FORTUNE 吉 was originally written 吉 and means *good fortune as foretold (▽ MOUTH) by a sage (± SCHOLAR).*

78   LONGEVITY 寿 originally written 壽, pictures *the praying (▽ MOUTH; ∋ HAND that makes gestures stressing request) for long life.* In addition, we see *HAIR* ⴹ *that has changed (MAN ⟨ and MAN-upside-down ⟩, i.e. a man that has changed his position) and wrinkles (* ⴹ *furrows).*

82   GOOD 善 was *dispute (言 WORDs) that is peacefully (ⴿ SHEEP) settled:* 善 .

85   LOVE 愛 consisted of several pictures and symbols to express this well-known feeling of affection, as follows. *To swallow 旡 [person ⟨ (see MAN) breathing in air ≋] affectionate feelings down in one's HEART* ❤ . At the bottom is the symbol 夂 , which means that *it is a lingering feeling (a person 刀 (see MAN) who slowly advances in spite of an obstacle ⌒):* 愛 .

NOTE: **GOOD LUCK SIGNS** has 10 characters (pp.12-13).
        There are 3 Phonograms (Dict. pp. 12-13).
        There are 2 Easy Characters (Lesson A, p. A12).
        There are 5 Not So Easy characters (above).

Do you still know the meanings of the two Easy Characters mentioned above and printed here? Please, go to **Lesson A**, p. A12 if you do not know both of them!

We now discuss Group **HUMAN BODY** . In Kanji

86 POWER 力 originally meaning STRENGTH was represented by *a picture of a muscle in its sheath:* 肕 .

92 SKIN 皮 is a picture of *the skin* 丿 *being stripped off by a hand* ㇈ *holding a knife* フ : 㾌 .

95 FOOT 足 was basicly the same writing, being *the foot with the ankle, heel and toes* 止 , *at rest* ○: 𠯢 (cp. PROCEED 辶).

96 BODY 身 was represented by *a person with a conspicuous abdomen:* 𠂤 .

97 FACE 面 was *the face* ◯ *with the nose* 自 *in the center:* 圙 .

98 STOMACH 胃 was represented by *the stomach* ⊗ *containing food* ∴ . (*The Radical FLESH* 肉 *was added,* because most parts of the human body carries FLESH as the Radical.): 胃 .

99 BONE 骨 was a picture of *a human skeleton:* 骨 .

101 NOSE 鼻 was *the nose* 自 *put on the body* 畀 *(the body* ⊕ *on legs* 八 *):* 鼻 .

NOTE: **HUMAN BODY** has 17 characters (Dict. pp.14-15).
There are 2 Phonograms (Dict. pp. 14-15).
There are 7 Easy Characters (Lesson A, p. A4).
There are 8 Not So Easy characters (above).

Do you still know the meanings of the Easy Characters mentioned above and printed here?
Please, go to **Lesson A**, p. A4 if you do not know all of them!

| 耳 |
口	手
舌	毛
目	心

B11

The next Group is | **INSTITUTIONS** |.

104 **MEETING** 会 was originally written: 會 : *a meeting* (△ *three lines coming together) where words* 日 *(SPEAK) are spoken at the fireside (* ⊕ *smoke outlet):* 會 .

105 **OFFICE** 局 , *a place where many people work, where words (* 口 *MOUTH) are spoken and many hands (repre-sented by the span* ⌐ *of the hand of a MAN* ⼕ : 尺 *):* 局 .

108 **COUNTRY** 国 was originally written 國 : *a country* ◯ *with its capital* ○ *, which must be defended by weapons* 戈 *(HALBERD):* 國 .

112 **FLOWER** 華, also meaning **CHINA**, pictured by *leaves and flowers on a branch* 🌿 *that are expanding* 于 *(breath* 丿 *that expands freely* 一 *after passing through an obstacle* 一 *) into full bloom:* 華 .

NOTE: **INSTITUTIONS** has 14 characters (Dict. pp.16-17).
There are 6 Phonograms (Dict. pp. 16-17).
There are 4 Easy Characters (Lesson A, p. A9).
There are 4 Not So Easy characters (above).

Do you still know the meanings of the Easy Characters mentioned above and printed here?
Please, go to **Lesson A**, p. A9 if you
do not know all of them!

Attention, please!
For Phonograms see **Lesson C** - Difficult characters.

Next Group is **LOCATIONS** .

120 **DIVISION, SECTOR (OF A CITY)** 区 was original-
ly written 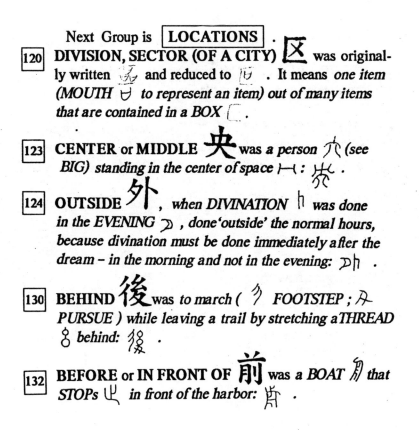 and reduced to 匹 . It means *one item*
(MOUTH 日 *to represent an item) out of many items*
that are contained in a BOX 匚 .

123 **CENTER or MIDDLE** 央 was *a person* 大 *(see*
BIG) standing in the center of space 冂 : 夬 .

124 **OUTSIDE** 外, *when DIVINATION* 卜 *was done*
in the EVENING 夕 , *done 'outside' the normal hours,*
because divination must be done immediately after the
dream – in the morning and not in the evening: 夕卜 .

130 **BEHIND** 後 was *to march (* 彳 *FOOTSTEP ;* 夊
PURSUE) while leaving a trail by stretching a THREAD
幺 *behind:* 後 .

132 **BEFORE or IN FRONT OF** 前 was *a BOAT* 舟 *that*
STOPs 止 *in front of the harbor:* 歬 .

NOTE: **LOCATIONS** has 16 characters (Dict. pp.18-20).
       There is 1 Phonogram (Dict. pp. 18-20).
       There are 10 Easy Characters (Lesson A, p. A10).
       There are 5 Not So Easy characters (above).

Do you still know the meanings of the Easy Characters mentioned above and printed here?
Please, go to **Lesson A**, p. A10 if you
do not know all of them!

上	中
下	左
南	北	内	右
		東	西

We will come now to the Group | **MISCELLANEOUS** | .

135 **STAND, PLATFORM** 台 was *a mound of earth (坐 grass) used as a look-out platform* 冂 : 高 .

136 **CHARACTER, LETTER** 字 *a character is the result of careful mixing of writing-units – a CHILD* 子 *must be carefully reared in the house* 冖 *(DWELLING):* 字 .

138 **FRAGRANCE** 香 was *the SWEET* 曰 *odor of fermented (* 八 *vapors) GRAIN* 禾 : 香 .

139 **RIGHT, JUST** 是 *just like the SUN* 曰 *seems to STOP* 止 *right above the equator* — : 是 .

140 **TRUTH** 真 *when TEN* 十 *EYEs* 目 *are looking at something on a pedestal* 兀 *and finding nothing is wrong (∟ straight angle):* 眞 .

NOTE: **MISCELLANEOUS** has 11 characters (Dict. pp.21-22).
There are 4 Phonograms (Dict. pp. 21-22).
There are 2 Easy Characters (Lesson A, p. A14).
There are 5 Not So Easy characters (above).

Do you still know the meanings of the Easy Characters mentioned above and printed here?
Please, go to **Lesson A**, p. A14 if you do not know both of them!

田

不

The next Group is **NATURE** .

152 STONE 石 *a stone* ○ *in a cliff* ⌐ : 石 .

154 WORLD 世 . Original meaning: **GENERATION**, represented by *"thirty" (three TEN's* 十 *combined:* 卅 *), which was the average person's lifetime during ancient times.*

155 LIGHT 光 *FIRE* 火 *being carried by a person* 儿 *(MAN):* 光 .

157 ROCK 岩 *a rock* 石 *(STONE) that was part of a MOUNTAIN:* 屮 : 岩 .

160 SPRING (FOUNTAIN) 泉 *WATER* 水 *spouting up* | *and expanding evenly* 穴 : 泉 .

161 SEA 海 *the mother* 母 *(WOMAN* 女 *with breasts* 八 *added) of all (* 屮 *grass, to suggest "omnipresence") WATER* 水 : 海 .

163 STAR 星 *sublimated matter that is ascending* ∪ *from the EARTH* 土 *, to become stars* 品 : 星 .

164 WIND 風 *motion of air* 几 *and INSECT* 虫 *(it was believed that insects were born when the wind blew):* 風 .

167 SNOW 雪 *RAIN* 雨 *that has solidified into snow, and being held in one's HAND* 彐 : 雪 .

169 CLOUD 雲 *vapors* ∕ *of water that rise to the sky* = *and will later come as RAIN* 雨 : 雲 .

B15

170 LIGHTNING 電 *that which extends* ㇆ㇹ *from the RAIN* 雨 *and strikes down* ㇈ : 電 .

171 SILVER 銀 *Metal* 金 *(see GOLD) and* 艮 DEFIANCE, *suggesting that silver is malleable ('defies' the action of a hammer):* 銀 .

NOTE: **NATURE** has 28 characters (Dict. pp.23-26).
There are 4 Phonograms (Dict. pp. 23-26).
There are 12 Easy Characters (Lesson A, p. A 6-7).
There are 12 Not So Easy characters (above).

Do you still know the meanings of the Easy Characters mentioned above and printed here?
Please, go to **Lesson A**, p. A 6-7 if you
do not know all of them!

火	日	
氷	月	
雨	天	山
島	土	川
金		水

Attention, please!
For Phonograms see **Lesson C** - Difficult characters.

The next Group is NUMBERS .

183 THOUSAND 千 *ten* 十 *platoons of men* (勹 *MAN), i.e. one thousand men:* 𠂤 .

184 TEN THOUSAND 万 . *Originally:* 萬 . *Picture of a scorpion, with its head* ⊗ *, its legs and tail* 𠂆 *, and its 'thousands' of claws:* 𢒉 : 萬 .

187 TWIN 双 *Originally:* 雙 . *One HAND* 彐 *holding two BIRDs* 隹 : 雙 .

188 HALF 半 *an OX* 牛 *split into two equal portions, namely split by cutting it lengthwise, the way that butchers normally do:* 半 .

189 NUMBER 号 *a statement (* 丂 *breath) coming out from the MOUTH* 口 : 号 .

190 EVERY 每 *grass* 屮 *, which can be found everywhere, and mother* * 𣎳 *, which gives the idea of fertility and abundance* 每 . * *(See in SEA No. 161.)*

191 TOGETHER 共 *twenty* 廿 *(two TENs* ++ *connected) HANDs* 廾 *joined together as if being done in a joined effort:* 共 .

192 UNIT (FOR COUNTING SHIPS) 隻 *a HAND* 彐 *that is holding one BIRD* 隹 : 隻 .

193 RANK 第 *a thread* 弓 *that is being wound around a BAMBOO* 竹 *spool* 丫 *, which gives to us the idea of succession:* 第 .

194 HOW MANY / MUCH 幾 *a guard [MAN 𠂉 with a spear 戈 (HALBERD)] listening to the slightest (幺 THREAD) movements:* 𢆷 .

195 NUMBER, COUNT 数 *to watch over (a HAND 彐 holding a stick ㅏ) women prisoners (𡚦 WOMAN locked 中 in prison 囗.)* 數攴 .

NOTE: **NUMBERS** has 24 characters (Dict. pp. 27-29).
　　　　There is only 1 Phonogram (Dict. pp. 27-29).
　　　　There are 12 Easy Characters (Lesson A, p. A 3).
　　　　There are 11 Not So Easy characters (above).

　　　Do you still know the meanings of the Easy Characters mentioned above and printed here?
Please, go to **Lesson A**, p. A 3 if you do not know all of them!

一	五	九
二	六	十
三	七	多
四	八	少

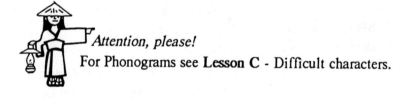

Attention, please!
For Phonograms see **Lesson C** - Difficult characters.

The next Group is OBJECTS .

197 DISH 皿 *a dish mounted on a pedestal, as used during banquets:* 豆 .

198 JEWEL 玉 *the precious gem • that only kings* 王 *(the mediator | between Heaven ‾ , Earth __ and Man ‾) could possess:* 玉 .

200 CLOTHING 衣 *a robe and its sleeves* ㇏ *and* ㇒ *its dragging over the floor:* 衣 .

203 PICTURE 画 . *Originally:* 畫 . *A HAND* ㇐ *holding a sylus | drawing a line — on a drawing board* ∧ , *and* 囲 *[the resulting drawing* ⊕ *put in a frame* ⊐ *]:* 畫 .

204 DRESS 服 *Etymology?*

206 SURFACE 表 *the hairy (* ⻖ *HAIR) outside of a fur coat (* 衣 *CLOTHES) , which revealed the function of the imperial huntsman:* 表 .

208 MEASURE; –METER (suffix) 計 *(Orig. meaning: TO CALCULATE) to be able to pronounce (* 言 *WORDS) the numbers ONE (—) to TEN (* 十 *), which was the minimal requirement for a person in order to be able to perform calculations:* 言十 .

210 SEAT 席 *mats (* 巾 *CLOTH) upon which the guests sat during ancient times' banquets [* 广 *SHELTER (house) ;* 廿 *= ++ = two TENs = many (guests)]:* 席 .

211 WRITING BRUSH 筆 *a BAMBOO* 竹 *writing brush (a HAND* ㇐ *holding a stylus | drawing a line — on a tablet* ∧ *):* 筆 .

B19

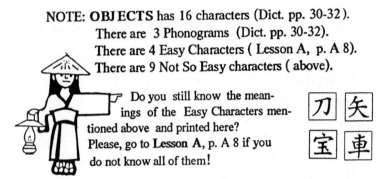

NOTE: **OBJECTS** has 16 characters (Dict. pp. 30-32).
There are 3 Phonograms (Dict. pp. 30-32).
There are 4 Easy Characters (Lesson A, p. A 8).
There are 9 Not So Easy characters (above).

Do you still know the meanings of the Easy Characters mentioned above and printed here?
Please, go to **Lesson A,** p. A 8 if you
do not know all of them!

Attention, please!
For Phonograms see **Lesson C** - Difficult characters.

The next Group is PERSONS .

217 HUSBAND 夫 *an adult person* 大 *(see MAN) who has a pin ─ in his hair, wearing the pin as a token of maturity:* 夫 .

219 MR. (lit. suffix) 氏 *representing a floating plant ⊂ that multiplies and grows in abundance:* ⊆ . *[Orig. meaning: "clan", "familiy".]*

220 PUBLIC 公 *division* 八 *and distribution of a private possession (* ○ *cocoon; with the self-enclosed silkworm it gives the idea of privacy):* 公 .

222 PEOPLE 民 *weed that grows in abundance (* ↓ *and* ∅ *are the small stems and leaves):* 民 .

223 ONESELF 自 *the NOSE* 自 *, representing the entire body of the person.*

225 DOCTOR (MEDICAL) 医 . *Originally:* 醫 . *Taking out* 殳 *(HAND* ∃ *making a jerky motion* ⌐ *) an ARROW* 矢 *from the receptacle* ⌐ *, in order to shoot down the demon, and to give elixir (* 酉 *WINE JUG) to the patient:* 醫 .

227 MAN 男 *the one that gives his STRENGTH* 力 *in the FIELD* ⊕ *. (The woman doing her work inside the house.):* 男 .

228 MR. (fam. suffix) 君 *a HAND* ∃ *holding a scepter* / *, and a MOUTH* ⊔ *that gives orders to people:* 君 . *[Orig. meaning: "ruler", "prince".]*

229 WIFE 妻 *the WOMAN* 女 *who holds (* ∃ *HAND) the duster* Ψ : 妻 .

B21

NOTE: **PESONS** has 19 characters (Dict. pp. 33-35).
There are 2 Phonograms (Dict. pp. 33-35).
There are 8 Easy Characters (Lesson A, p. A4-5).
There are 9 Not So Easy characters (above).

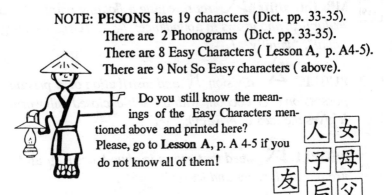

Do you still know the meanings of the Easy Characters mentioned above and printed here?
Please, go to **Lesson A**, p. A 4-5 if you
do not know all of them!

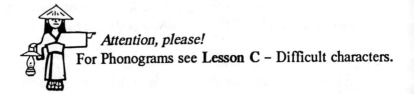

Attention, please!
For Phonograms see **Lesson C** – Difficult characters.

The next Group is $\boxed{\text{SIZE}}$.

233 **BIG, FAT** 太 *a person with outstretched arms as if showing the size of a large object; with a "dot"* • *added in order to distinguish it from* 大 **BIG** (No. 231): 太 .

234 **LARGE, HUGE** 巨 *a large carpenter's square* 工 *which has a handle* コ : 巨 .

235 **LONG** 長 *hair* 彡 *so long that it is tied with a band* — *and a brooch* Y : 昪 .

236 **CORDIAL, THICK** 厚 *generosity expressed by* ⊖ *a gift coming down* ⌐ *from above* (⌼ *gift received):* .

238 **SHORT** 短 *a dart (small arrow)* 矢 *and a platter-on-a-pedestal* 豆 , *i.e. two short utensils:* 矢豆.

NOTE: SIZE has 8 characters (Dict. p. 36).
There is no Phonogram (Dict. pp. 36).
There are 3 Easy Characters (Lesson A, p. A13).
There are 5 Not So Easy characters (above).

Do you still know the meanings of the Easy Characters mentioned above and printed here?
Please, go to **Lesson A**, p. A 13 if you do not know all of them!

小 大
高

The next Group is TIME .

239 **AGAIN** 又 *the right HAND* ㄨ *, which is being used 'again and again'. (The left HAND* ㄓ *being rarely used, unless the person is left-handed.)*

240 **LONG TIME** 久 *a person* ㄇ *(see MAN) who is meeting an obstacle* ヽ *during his walk:* 久 .

242 **MINUTE** 分 *a KNIFE* ㄅ *divides an object into two small portions* 八 : 川 .

243 **NOW** 今 *the time that follows* ㄱ *the past* △ *which was the time that has come full circle (three lines that have met each other):* 今 .

247 **LONG TIME** 永 *veins of water in the Earth flowing incessanty:* 川 .

248 **OLD** 古 *when it has passed from MOUTH* 口 *to mouth for many (* 十 *TEN) generations:* 古 .

249 **NOT YET** 未 *a TREE* 木 *not yet fully grown; i.e. the top portion of which is not yet fully developed:* 未 .

250 **YEAR** 年 *the time it takes to harvest all the GRAIN* 禾 *[thousand* � *(see* **THOUSAND,** *No. 183) grains']:* 秊 .

252 **AGAIN** 再 *a second* 二 *(TWO) weighing on a weighing scale* 一 : 再 .

254 **NEXT** 次 *to take breath* 㐱 *(BREATHE) one after another (* 二 *TWO):* 二㐱 .

B24

255 | **IMMEDIATE** 即 soup 皀 *(a pot* ⊖ *and* ㇄ *a spoon)* and a soup ladle 卩 next to it, i.e. soup that can be immediately consumed: 𝕰𝕻·

259 | **AUTUMN** 秋 when the GRAIN 禾 in the field ripens and attains a fiery 火 *(FIRE)* color: 禾火·

260 | **DAYTIME, NOON** 昼 . Originally: 晝 . Time frame □ in which there is light (⊖ *SUN) for people to write (STYLUS)* 聿 : 晝 .

261 | **TIME** 時 the SUN ⊖ and to measure [i.e. 'to measure the pulse' 寸 *(the place on the HAND* 又 *indicated by the dash* − *)]the growth of plants* 止 : 時 .

264 | **MORNING** 朝 the SUN ⊙ rising 一 behind mangrove trees 木 *(tree* ψ *with its branches going down and striking roots in the ground* 入 *) as seen from a BOAT* 月 : 朝 .

NOTE: **TIME** has 28 characters (Dict. p. 37-40).
There are 5 Phonograms (Dict. pp. 37-40).
There are 8 Easy Characters (Lesson A, p. A9).
There are 15 Not So Easy characters (above).

Do you still know the meanings of the Easy Characters mentioned above and printed here?
Please, go to **Lesson A, p. A 9** if you do not know all of them!

夕	夜	春
午	月	夏
早	冬	

Attention, please!
For Phonograms see **Lesson C** – Difficult characters.

The next Group is $\boxed{\text{TRAVEL}}$.

269 **GO** 行 *footsteps made by left and right feet:* 彳彳 .

271 **ARRIVE AT** 到 *a bird with wings backward* Ψ *flying downwards and reaching the EARTH:* Ψ .*

273 **JOURNEY** 旅 *men* 𠂉𠂉 *(see MAN) on a journey, finding shelter under the overhanging branches* ⌐ *of a tree* 屮 *(see TREE) during bad weather:* 𣃴 .

274 **NAVIGATION** 航 *a BOAT* 舟 *and the navigator resolutely standing on both legs* 亢 *:* 舩 .

276 **PLAY** 遊 *to PROCEED* 辵 *and* 𠂆 *(a person with arms making fluttering motions, swimming aimlessly) and* 子 *(CHILD):* 遊 .

* The original pronunciation of this character was **Tao⁴**. The unit 刂 **Tao¹** is here 'phonetic', to give the pronunciation of the character.

NOTE: **TRAVEL** has 10 characters (Dict. p. 41-42).
There is no Phonogram (Dict. pp. 41-42).
There are 5 Easy Characters (Lesson A, p. A11-12).
There are 5 Not So Easy characters (above).

Do you still know the meanings of the Easy Characters mentioned above and printed here?
Please, go to **Lesson A**, p. A 11-12 if you do not know all of them!

至	出
舟	飛
船	

The next Group is VEGETATION .

281 BEANS 豆 *a simple meal of beans* • *served on a stemmed platter:* 豆 .

282 FLOWER 花 *the portion of plants* ΨΨ *that has greatly changed* 刀乚 *[a person* 刀 *(MAN) and* 乚 *person-upside-down, i.e. a person who has "changed" position]:* ΨΨ 刀乚 .

NOTE: **VEGETATION** has 9 characters (Dict. p. 43).
There is 1 Phonogram (Dict. p. 43).
There are 6 Easy Characters (Lesson A, p. A6).
There are 2 Not So Easy characters (above).

Do you still know the meanings of the Easy Characters mentioned above and printed here?
Please, go to **Lesson A**, p. A6 if you
do not know all of them!

木	瓜
本	林
果	竹

Attention, please!
For Phonograms see **Lesson C** – Difficult characters.

288 STOP 止 *the foot-at-rest, showing the heel* ∟ *, the toe* ⌐ *and the ankle* Ʋ *of a foot:* 屮 .

290 LEAVE 去 *an empty vessel* ∪ *; its content has been taken away and its lid* 大 *put back:* 古 .

291 WRAP (v) 包 *a foetus "wrapped" in the womb:* 𓂸 .

292 ADD 加 *STRENGTH* 力 *"added" to one's speech* (口 *MOUTH):* 力口 .

293 REST 休 *a person* 𠆳 *(MAN) who is resting under a TREE* 木 *:* 𠆳木 .

299 COMPLETION 完 *putting head gear* 一 *on a person* 儿 *(see MAN) completes a person's dressing and putting a roof on a house* 宀 *(DWELLING) completes the house:* 家 .

300 WALK 步 *to go "step by step", namely, to "move"* 屮 *[the mirror image of* 止 *(STOP)] and to STOP* 止 *consecutively:* 㣇 .

301 TAKE 取 *a HAND* 彐 *is holding an EAR* 𦥑 *:* 𦥑彐 .

302 RECEIVE 受 *one hand* 爫 *transferring* ⌐ *an object to another person's HAND* 彐 *:* 𠬛 .

303 KNOW 知 *to know how to speak (* 口 *MOUTH) with precision (an arrow that hits the mark* 矢 *):* 矢口 .

B28

295 RUN 走 *a person with the head bent downward* 夨 *who runs* 止 *(foot, see STOP) quickly:* 走 .

305 STUDY; SCHOOL 学 *Originally:* 學 *.The CHILD* 子 *in darkness (* ∩ *small room) and the two hands* 臼 *of the master pouring knowledge* ⚊ *to the child:* 學 .

307 SEND 送 *to PROCEED* 辵 *in the dark carrying a torch* (火 *FIRE held by a pair of HANDS* 廾 *):* 送 .

308 WRITE 書 *a STYLUS* 聿 *and the drawing* ⊕ *made by it:* 書 .

309 GET UP 起 *putting oneSELF* 己 *in motion* 走 *(RUN):* 起 .

314 PROHIBIT 禁 *bad omen* 示 *(see REVELATION) from TREES* 林 *:* 禁 .

315 DEMAND 需 *plants must have RAIN* 雨 *in order to develop in full [only the roots* 而 *of the plants are shown, the top portions are left out]:* 需 .

NOTE: **VERBS** has 30 characters (Dict. p. 44-47).
There is 1 Phonogram (Dict. p. 44-47).
There are 12 Easy Characters (Lesson A, p. A13-14).
There are 17 Not So Easy characters (above).

Do you still know the meanings of the Easy Characters mentioned above and printed here?
Please, go to **Lesson A**, p. A13-14 if you do not know all of them!

来	言
問	見

引	立	開	看
入	回	閉	押

℞eview 1 (Lesson B)

The ⎡Review I⎤ Tables on pages B32 to B34 will help you to obtain knowledge of all Not-So-Easy characters in Lesson B. *All characters are accompanied by their ancestral forms* to help you to remember their meanings.

Hi-lite or *circle* all the characters whose meanings you know. This allows to see all the ones that you *do not* know. Please, go back and study them again until you know all of them.

After you have finished working on above Review Tables, you should go to ⎡Review II⎤ on pages B35 to B43. Here you find Review Tables with characters *not accompanied by their ancestral forms.*

Warning - avoid getting fines! If this book is a book from the Library, *do not hi-lite or circle in this book!* Make first copies of the pages that you need and hi-lite or circle there!

1	丸	**7**	老	**10**	良	**14**	亮
15	若	**17**	強	**18**	悪	**20**	寒
21	新	**22**	寡	**23**	麗	**26**	虫
28	貝	**29**	虎	**31**	竜	**33**	豚
35	鹿	**36**	熊	**38**	戸	**42**	屋
51	色	**52**	赤	**53**	青	**59**	司
60	加	**64**	商	**68**	業	**71**	卵
72	茶	**76**	平	**77**	吉	**78**	寿
82	善	**85**	愛	**86**	力	**92**	皮
95	足	**96**	身	**97**	面	**98**	胃
99	骨	**101**	鼻	**104**	会	**105**	局
108	国	**112**	華	**120**	区	**123**	央
124	外	**130**	後	**132**	前	**135**	台
136	字	**138**	香	**139**	是	**140**	真
152	石	**154**	世	**155**	光	**157**	岩

160	泉	161	海	163	星	164	風
167	雪	169	雲	170	電	171	銀
183	千	184	万	187	双	188	半
189	号	190	每	191	共	192	隻
193	第	194	幾	195	数	197	皿
198	玉	200	衣	203	画	204	服 *Etymology*
206	表	208	計	210	席	211	筆
217	夫	219	氏	220	公	222	民
223	自	225	医	227	男	228	君
229	妻	233	太	234	巨	235	長
236	厚	238	短	239	又	240	久
242	分	243	今	247	永	248	古
249	未	250	年	252	再	254	次
255	即	259	秋	260	昼	261	時
264	朝	269	行	271	到	273	旅

274	航 舢	276	遊 遊	281	豆 豆	282	花 苁
288	止 止	290	去 杏	291	包 包	292	加 加
293	休 伙	299	完 完	300	步 步	301	取 取
302	受 受	303	知 知	295	走 奄	305	学 學
307	送 送	308	書 書	309	起 起	314	禁 禁
315	需 需						

Review 11 (Lesson B)

In the following Review Tables, the characters are *not* accompanied by their ancestral forms. You should be able to know the characters without them.

Take first | Review No. 1 | and *hi-lite* or *circle* all the characters that you know already. This allows you to see the characters that you *do not* know. You now go back to Lesson B and study the unknown characters again.

After a day or two, you take | Review No. 2 | and follow the same procedure. There should be more known characters on Review No. 2 than on Review No. 1 .

After Review No.2, you take | Review No. 3 | and if necessary also | Review No. 4 | . You should now know all characters of Lesson B.

Warning - avoid getting fines! If this book is a book from the Library, *do not hi-lite or circle in this book!* Make first copies of the pages that you need and hi-lite or circle there!

1	丸	7	老	10	良	14	亮	160	泉
15	若	17	強	18	悪	20	寒	167	雪
21	新	22	寡	23	麗	26	虫	183	千
28	貝	29	虎	31	竜	33	豚	189	号
35	鹿	36	熊	38	戸	42	屋	193	第
51	色	52	赤	53	青	59	司	198	玉
60	加	64	商	68	業	71	卵	206	表
72	茶	76	平	77	吉	78	寿	217	夫
82	善	85	愛	86	力	92	皮	223	自
95	足	96	身	97	面	98	胃	229	妻
99	骨	101	鼻	104	会	105	局	236	厚
108	国	112	華	120	区	123	央	242	分
124	外	130	後	132	前	135	台	249	未
136	字	138	香	139	是	140	真	255	即
152	石	154	世	155	光	157	岩	264	朝

161 海	163 星	164 風	274 航	309 起
169 雲	170 電	171 銀	288 止	282 花
184 万	187 双	188 半	293 休	292 加
190 毎	191 共	192 隻	302 受	301 取
194 幾	195 数	197 皿	307 送	305 学
200 衣	203 画	204 服	315 需	314 禁
208 計	210 席	211 筆	276 遊	
219 氏	220 公	222 民	290 去	
225 医	227 男	228 君	299 完	
233 太	234 巨	235 長	303 知	
238 短	239 又	240 久	308 書	
243 今	247 永	248 古	281 豆	
250 年	252 再	254 次	291 包	
259 秋	260 昼	261 時	300 歩	
269 行	271 到	273 旅	295 走	

1	丸	7	老	10	良	14	亮	160	泉
15	若	17	強	18	悪	20	寒	167	雪
21	新	22	寡	23	麗	26	虫	183	千
28	貝	29	虎	31	竜	33	豚	189	号
35	鹿	36	熊	38	戸	42	屋	193	第
51	色	52	赤	53	青	59	司	198	玉
60	加	64	商	68	業	71	卵	206	表
72.	茶	76	平	77	吉	78	寿	217	夫
82	善	85	愛	86	力	92	皮	223	自
95	足	96	身	97	面	98	胃	229	妻
99	骨	101	鼻	104	会	105	局	236	厚
108	国	112	華	120	区	123	央	242	分
124	外	130	後	132	前	135	台	249	未
136	字	138	香	139	是	140	真	255	即
152	石	154	世	155	光	157	岩	264	朝

B38

REVIEW No. 2 A

161	海	163	星	164	風	274	航	309	起
169	雲	170	電	171	銀	288	止	282	花
184	万	187	双	188	半	293	休	292	加
190	毎	191	共	192	隻	302	受	301	取
194	幾	195	数	197	皿	307	送	305	学
200	衣	203	画	204	服	315	需	314	禁
208	計	210	席	211	筆	276	遊		
219	氏	220	公	222	民	290	去		
225	医	227	男	228	君	299	完		
233	太	234	巨	235	長	303	知		
238	短	239	又	240	久	308	書		
243	今	247	永	248	古	281	豆		
250	年	252	再	254	次	291	包		
259	秋	260	昼	261	時	300	歩		
269	行	271	到	273	旅	295	走		

1	丸	7	老	10	良	14	亮	160	泉
15	若	17	強	18	悪	20	寒	167	雪
21	新	22	寨	23	麗	26	虫	183	千
28	貝	29	虎	31	竜	33	豚	189	号
35	鹿	36	熊	38	戸	42	屋	193	第
51	色	52	赤	53	青	59	司	198	玉
60	加	64	商	68	業	71	卵	206	表
72.	茶	76	平	77	吉	78	寿	217	夫
82	善	85	愛	86	力	92	皮	223	自
95	足	96	身	97	面	98	胃	229	妻
99	骨	101	鼻	104	会	105	局	236	厚
108	国	112	華	120	区	123	央	242	分
124	外	130	後	132	前	135	台	249	未
136	字	138	香	139	是	140	真	255	即
152	石	154	世	155	光	157	岩	264	朝

REVIEW No. 3 A

161	海	163	星	164	風	274	航	309	起
169	雲	170	電	171	銀	288	止	282	花
184	万	187	双	188	半	293	休	292	加
190	毎	191	共	192	隻	302	受	301	取
194	幾	195	数	197	皿	307	送	305	学
200	衣	203	画	204	服	315	需	314	禁
208	計	210	席	211	筆	276	遊		
219	氏	220	公	222	民	290	去		
225	医	227	男	228	君	299	完		
233	太	234	巨	235	長	303	知		
238	短	239	又	240	久	308	書		
243	今	247	永	248	古	281	豆		
250	年	252	再	254	次	291	包		
259	秋	260	昼	261	時	300	歩		
269	行	271	到	273	旅	295	走		

1	丸	7	老	10	良	14	亮	160	泉

1	丸	7	老	10	良	14	亮	160	泉
15	若	17	強	18	悪	20	寒	167	雪
21	新	22	寮	23	麗	26	虫	183	千
28	貝	29	虎	31	竜	33	豚	189	号
35	鹿	36	熊	38	戸	42	屋	193	第
51	色	52	赤	53	青	59	司	198	玉
60	加	64	商	68	業	71	卵	206	表
72	茶	76	平	77	吉	78	寿	217	夫
82	善	85	愛	86	力	92	皮	223	自
95	足	96	身	97	面	98	胃	229	妻
99	骨	101	鼻	104	会	105	局	236	厚
108	国	112	華	120	区	123	央	242	分
124	外	130	後	132	前	135	台	249	未
136	字	138	香	139	是	140	真	255	即
152	石	154	世	155	光	157	岩	264	朝

161	海	163	星	164	風	274	航	309	起
169	雲	170	電	171	銀	288	止	282	花
184	万	187	双	188	半	293	休	292	加
190	毎	191	共	192	隻	302	受	301	取
194	幾	195	数	197	皿	307	送	305	学
200	衣	203	画	204	服	315	需	314	禁
208	計	210	席	211	筆	276	遊		
219	氏	220	公	222	民	290	去		
225	医	227	男	228	君	299	完		
233	太	234	巨	235	長	303	知		
238	短	239	又	240	久	308	書		
243	今	247	永	248	古	281	豆		
250	年	252	再	254	次	291	包		
259	秋	260	昼	261	時	300	歩		
269	行	271	到	273	旅	295	走		

REVIEW No. 4 B

Lesson C
Difficult Kanji

About 15% of all Kanji characters in this book are dificult to learn. As mentioned in the **Introduction**, there are two kinds of characters. The original characters were pictures from which the meanings of the characters were derived. They were written with a stylus on bones, shells, etc. *There are only a couple of thousand of them known today.* **Lessons A and B contain such characters.** They are called **"Pictograms"** (*picto* = picture; *gram* = writing).

As time went by, more and more characters were needed. *The new characters, however, were no pictures. One reason was the use of the writing brush, invented by a Chinese general, who needed a faster way of writing his reports at the end of the day.* It was easier and faster to write with a brush using ink and paper than to carve pictures on bones, shells, etc. *However, the brush writings were only approximations of the original stylus drawings, because unlike the stylus, the brush could not make the intricate loops and details of the stylus drawings.*

A new method of creating characters was now used. A new character was a combination of two existing writing units. One unit indicated *to what group the characters belonged;* it is called the *"Radical"* (*radix* = root). The other unit *referred to its (Chinese) pronuniation,* and is called the *"Phonetic"* (*phono* = sound).; no pictures were introduced to indicate which character it really was. Lesson C contains such characters. They are called "Phonograms" (*phono* = sound; *gram* = writing).

From the foregoing it follows that we have to simply memorize the meanings of the characters in Lesson C.

A proven method to learn the meaning of a foreign word is to **write down the word several times in a row while pronouncing its meaning.** The chapter **"How to Write a Kanji Character"** which appears in the **Appendix** tells you how to write a Kanji character.

The Radical tells us to which group the character belongs and it sometimes can be very helpful to us in knowing which character it is. Here are some examples:

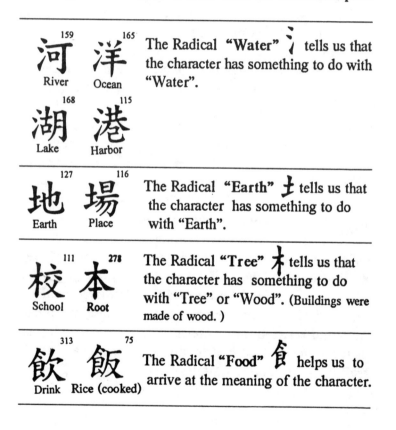

159 河 River   165 洋 Ocean   The Radical "Water" シ tells us that the character has something to do with "Water".

168 湖 Lake   115 港 Harbor

127 地 Earth   116 場 Place   The Radical "Earth" 土 tells us that the character has something to do with "Earth".

111 校 School   278 本 Root   The Radical "Tree" 木 tells us that the character has something to do with "Tree" or "Wood". (Buildings were made of wood.)

313 飲 Drink   75 飯 Rice (cooked)   The Radical "Food" 食 helps us to arrive at the meaning of the character.

List of Difficult characters

円 58 Yen	正 3 Correct	百 182 Hundred	地 127 Earth	低 8 Low	冷 9 Cool	私 226 I
町 106 Town	空 137 Sky	杯 202 Cup	店 39 Shop	房 40 Room	所 109 Place	物 205 Object
河 159 River	皇 230 Emperor	界 162 World	洋 165 Ocean	昨 258 Yester-	紙 209 Paper	校 111 School
祥 79 Good fortune	特 141 Special	値 63 Price	薬 285 Medicine	都 113 Metropolis	週 263 Week	眼 100 Eye
郵 142 Mail	港 115 Harbor	貸 67 Lend	飲 313 Drink	階 47 Story. Floor	飯 75 Rice	場 116 Place
晩 265 Evening	湖 168 Lake	運 80 Luck	福 84 Good fortune	歳 266 Year old	楼 48 Tall building	緑 56 Green
語 143 Language	館 49 Building	頭 102 Head	鶏 37 Chicken	**REVIEW No. 1**		

Warning - avoid stiff fines! Do not hi-lite or circle in this book if this book is a book from the Library; make copies first and hi-lite or circle there!

73

List of Difficult characters

円 [58]	正 [3]	百 [182]	地 [127]	低 [8]	冷 [9]	私 [226]
Yen	Correct	Hundred	Earth	Low	Cool	I
町 [106]	空 [137]	杯 [202]	店 [39]	房 [40]	所 [109]	物 [205]
Town	Sky	Cup	Shop	Room	Place	Object
河 [159]	皇 [230]	界 [162]	洋 [165]	昨 [258]	紙 [209]	校 [111]
River	Emperor	World	Ocean	Yester-	Paper	School
祥 [79]	特 [141]	値 [63]	薬 [285]	都 [113]	週 [263]	眼 [100]
Good fortune	Special	Price	Medicine	Metropolis	Week	Eye
郵 [142]	港 [115]	貸 [67]	飲 [313]	階 [47]	飯 [75]	場 [116]
Mail	Harbor	Lend	Drink	Story, Floor	Rice	Place
晩 [265]	湖 [161]	運 [80]	福 [84]	歳 [266]	楼 [48]	緑 [56]
Evening	Lake	Luck	Good fortune	Year old	Tall building	Green
語 [143]	館 [49]	頭 [102]	鶏 [37]	REVIEW No. 2		
Language	Building	Head	Chicken			

Warning - avoid stiff fines! Do not hi-lite or circle in this book if this book is a book from the Library; make copies first and hi-lite or circle there!

C4

List of Difficult characters

円 [58] Yen	正 [3] Correct	百 [182] Hundred	地 [127] Earth	低 [8] Low	冷 [9] Cool	私 [226] I
町 [106] Town	空 [137] Sky	杯 [202] Cup	店 [39] Shop	房 [40] Room	所 [109] Place	物 [205] Object
河 [159] River	皇 [230] Emperor	界 [162] World	洋 [165] Ocean	昨 [258] Yester-	紙 [209] Paper	校 [111] School
祥 [79] Good fortune	特 [141] Special	値 [63] Price	薬 [285] Medicine	都 [113] Metropolis	週 [263] Week	眼 [100] Eye
郵 [142] Mail	港 [115] Harbor	貸 [67] Lend	飲 [313] Drink	階 [47] Story. Floor	飯 [75] Rice	場 [116] Place
晩 [265] Evening	湖 [168] Lake	運 [80] Luck	福 [84] Good fortune	歳 [266] Year old	楼 [48] Tall building	緑 [56] Green
語 [143] Language	館 [49] Building	頭 [102] Head	鶏 [37] Chicken	**REVIEW No. 3**		

Warning - avoid stiff fines! Do not hi-lite or circle in this book if this book is a book from the Library; make copies first and hi-lite or circle there!

C5

List of Difficult characters

円 58	正 3	百 182	地 127	低 8	冷 9	私 226
Yen	Correct	Hundred	Earth	Low	Cool	I
町 106	空 137	杯 202	店 39	房 40	所 109	物 205
Town	Sky	Cup	Shop	Room	Place	Object
河 159	皇 230	界 162	洋 165	昨 258	紙 209	校 111
River	Emperor	World	Ocean	Yester-	Paper	School
祥 79	特 141	値 63	薬 285	都 113	週 263	眼 100
Good fortune	Special	Price	Medicine	Metropolis	Week	Eye
郵 142	港 115	貸 67	飲 313	階 47	飯 75	場 116
Mail	Harbor	Lend	Drink	Story. Floor	Rice	Place
晩 265	湖 168	運 80	福 84	歳 266	楼 48	緑 56
Evening	Lake	Luck	Good fortune	Year old	Tall building	Green
語 143	館 49	頭 102	鶏 37	REVIEW No. 4		
Language	Building	Head	Chicken			

Warning - avoid stiff fines! Do not hi-lite or circle in this book if this book is a book from the Library; make copies first and hi-lite or circle there!

Dictionary

ADJECTIVES

1	丸 ³	GAN, *maru(i)* **round.** *A person* 刀 *(see MAN) rolling down a CLIFF* ˥ : 刃
2	甘 ⁵	KAN, *ama(i)* **sweet, indulgent.** *Something sweet* — *being held in the MOUTH* 口 : 甘.
3	正	SEI, SHO, *tada(shii)* **correct.** Phonogram: [Chêng⁴] = Rad. + 正 Chêng⁴ (Ph.127).
4	安 ⁶	AN **peace, calm;** *yasu(i)* **cheap.** *When a WOMAN* 女 *is inside the house (DWELL-ING):* 宀 : 安 .
5	好	KO, *kono(mu), su(ku)* **good; like (v), be fond of.** *When one has a wife (* 女 *WOMAN) and children* *(* 子 *CHILD):* 女 子.
6	全	ZEN, *matta(ku)* **complete(ly).** *The WORK* 工 *is completed* △ *(three lines joined* *together):* 全 .
7	老	RŌ, *o(iru/i), fu(keru)* **aged.** *HAIR* 毛 *that have changed in color (a person* 人 *(MAN)* *who has changed his position* 匕 *– is upside* *down):* 老 .
8	低 ⁷	TEI, *hiku(i)* **low, short.** Phonogram: [Ti¹] = Rad. + 氐 Ti¹ (Ph.349).

1

9	冷	REI, *hi(yasu/eru)*, *sa(masu/meru)* **cool.** Phonogram: [Leng³] = Rad. + 令 *Ling⁴* (Ph.438).
10	良	RYO, *i(i)*, *yo(i)* **good.** *A gift ⊖ coming down ⊢ from Heaven that should not be rejected (stopped ∟ in its fall ⼊):*
11	直 ⁸	CHOKU, JIKI, *nao(su/ru)* **straight.** *TEN + EYEs ⊕ looking and finding nothing is wrong (∟ straight angle):*
12	明	MEI, MYŌ, *aka(rui)* **bright.** *When the MOON 🌙 is shining through the window ⊘ , the room is brightly lit:*
13	美 ⁹	BI **beauty;** *utsuku(shii)* **beautiful.** *Beautiful, as is a big sheep (⼤ BIG; ⼨ SHEEP) with fully developed horns :*
14	亮	RYŌ, **clear;** *suke, aki.* *A person ⼈ (MAN) living in a capital city 京 (No. 107) who is more well-informed than one living outside:*
15	若	JAKU, NYAKU, *waka(i)* **young.** *To gather ⇒ edible (⼝ MOUTH) young herbs (ψψ GRASS) :*
16	弱 ¹⁰	JAKU, *yowa(i)* **weak;** *yowa(ru)* **grow weak.** *A young, 'weak' bird represented by its still fluffy feathers:*

2

17	強 [11]	KYŌ, GŌ, *tsuyo(i)* **strong.** *A beetle (see ⌇ INSECT) that bounces up in the air (弓 BOW) and falls on its back ᔆ :* 強 .
18	悪	AKU, O, *waru(i)* **bad, evil, wrong.** *Representing a HEART ♡ that is evil [the symbol for WORK 工 deformed into 亞):* 悪 .
19	貴 [12]	KI, *tatto(i)*, *tōto(i)* **noble, precious.** *A basket 釆 filled with money (貝 SHELL):* 貴 .
20	寒	KAN, *samu(i)* **midwinter, cold.** *A person 个 (MAN) who seeks protection against the freezing 冫 (ICE) weather by lying inside 冖 (DWELLING) straw 茻 :* 寒 .
21	新 [13]	SHIN, *atara(shii)* **new.** *To cut (斤 AXE) new branches from the TREE 木 , which were used to beat (辛 OFFEND) criminals:* 新 .
22	寡 [14]	KA **alone, widowed; few, small.** *Persons 頁 (HEAD) living in the same house 宀 (DWELLING) now separated 八 (刀 KNIFE that separates) from each other:* 寡 .
23	麗 [19]	REI, *uruwa(shii)* **beautiful, lovely.** *Representing beauty by a pair of beautiful earrings 丽 and a DEER 鹿 with beautiful antlers 屮屮 :* 麗 .

ANIMALS

24	牛 ⁴	**GYŪ**, *ushi* **ox, cow; cattle.** *Representing an ox (seen from behind): only the two hind legs and tail are seen* ✝ *; the head is shown with the horns* Ψ : ⵜ.
25	犬	**KEN**, *inu* **dog.** *A dog (seen from the front): showing its two front legs and its head (turned aside):* 犬.
26	虫 ⁶	**CHŪ**, *mushi* **insect.** *Picture of a worm or an insect:* ⌇.
27	羊	**YŌ**, *hitsuji* **sheep.** *Picture of a sheep (seen from behind): the horns* Ƴ *, four feet and a tail* ✝ : 羊.
28	貝 ⁷	*kai* **(sea) shell.** *Picture of a 'cowrie' shell, used as money in ancient China:* 貝.
29	虎 ⁸	**KO**, *tora* **tiger.** *Representing the stripes of the tiger:* 虎. *
30	馬 ¹⁰	**BA, MA**, *uma* **horse.** *Picture of a horse with its mane blowing in the wind:* 馬.
31	竜	**RYŪ, RYŌ** *tatsu* **dragon.** *Original writing:* 龍. *A dragon 龍 flying towards the sky (dragon* 竜 *, wings* 飛 *, and the sky* ⚏ *).* **

* The symbol 儿 (see MAN) is used here, because a tiger can stand up on two legs like a man.

** It was believed that dragons could fly towards the sky and thereby caused rain. (They were lying inside the well during the dry season.)

32	魚 11	GYO, *sakana, uo* **fish.** *Picture of a fish: head* ㅅ *, scaly body* ⊕ *, and tail* ⌒: 象 .
33	豚	TON, *buta* **pig.** *A suckling PIG* 豕 *, the FLESH* 肉 *of which is being consumed:* 肉豕.
34	鳥	CHŌ, *tori* **bird.** *A picture of a bird* 鳥 .
35	鹿	ROKU, *shika* **deer.** *Representing a deer* 鹿 *with its head* ∀ *and antlers* Ψ *, its body* 𠃊 *(see CORPSE) and its feet* ㅆ.
36	熊 14	YŪ, *kuma* **bear.** *Representing a bear:* 熊 *(* 𠯑 *head,* 肉 *body,* 彐 *claws, and* ⺣ *feet).*
37	鶏 19	KEI, *niwatori* **chicken.** Phonogram: [Chi¹] = Rad. + 奚 *Hsi¹* (Ph.881).

BUILDINGS

38	戸 4	KO, *to* **door.** *The left-hand leaf* 戸 *of a swinging-door* 門.
39	店 8	TEN, *mise* **shop.** Phonogram: [Tien⁴] = Rad. + 占 *Chan¹* (Ph.720).
40	房	BŌ, *fusa* **room.** Phonogram: [Fang¹] = Rad. + 方 Fang¹ (Ph.261).
41	門	MON, *kado* **gate, door.** *Picture of a saloon-door with swinging leaves:* 門.
42	屋 9	OKU, *ya* **house; shop, store.** *A place where a person* 尸 *(see CORPSE) can retreat* 至 *(* 至 *bird with wings backward coming down to the EARTH* 土 *):* 屋.
43	室	SHITSU **room.** *A building* 宀 *(DWELLING) to which one returns after work (* 至 *bird with wings backward, coming down to EARTH* 土 *):* 室.
44	宮 10	KYŪ, GŪ, KU, *miya* **palace; imperial.** *Imperial represented by the imperial palace: a DWELLING* 宀 *containing a series of rooms* 呂 *:* 宮.
45	家	KA, KE, *ie, ya* **house, home, household.** *A DWELLING* 宀 *where PIGs* 豕 *have free entry. (To make sure that they were adequately fed, pigs had the same privileges as dogs today):* 家.

46	堂 [11]	DŌ **hall.** *A building [宀 (DWELLING), crest 丷, and ○ window] where soil 土 (EARTH) is sheltered:* 堂 .
47	階 [12]	KAI **story, floor; step, grade.** Phonogram: [Chieh¹] = Rad. + 皆 Chieh¹ (Ph.319).
48	楼 [13]	RŌ **tower, tall building.** *Originally:* 樓 . Phonogram: [Lou²] = Rad. + 婁 Lou² (Ph.790).
49	館 [16]	KAN **building.** Phonogram: [Kuan³]: Rad. + 官 Kuan¹ (Ph.751).

COLORS

50	白 5	HAKU, *shiro* **white.** *The sun ⊙ just rising above the horizon, causing the sky to become "white"*: ⊖ .
51	色 6	SHOKU, SHIKI, *iro* **color.** *A MAN ? with a red (color of a SEAL P) face*: 色 .
52	赤 7	SEKI, SHAKU, *aka, aka(i)* **red.** *Representing an angry man 大 (see BIG) his face turning red (火 FIRE)*: 赤 .
53	青 8	SEI, SHŌ, *ao, ao(i)* **blue; green.** *The color (凵 crucible containing substance • colored by heat) of plants 屮 emerging from the EARTH 土 :* 青 .
54	黒 11	KOKU, *kuro, kuro(i)* **black.** *Soot ⊃c deposited by a smoky FIRE 炎 around a vent ⊕ :* 黒 .
55	黄	KŌ, Ō, *ki* **yellow.** *The fiery glow 炗 (a MAN 人 carrying a torch 艹) from the FIELDs ⊕ :* 黄 .
56	緑 14	RYOKU, ROKU, *midori* **green.** Phonogram: [Lu⁴] = Rad. + 录 Lu⁴ (Ph.525).

8

ENTERPRISE

57	工 ³	KŌ, KU **work, construction.** *The ancient carpenter's square to symbolize 'work':* 工 .
58	円 ⁴	EN **yen**; *maru(i)* **round, circular.** *Originally:* 圓 . Phonogram: [Yüan²] = Rad.+ 員 Yüan² (Phonetic).
59	司 ⁵	SHI **control, manage.** *A person* 𠆢 *(MAN) bending over* �](to shout (⼝ MOUTH) his orders:* 司 .
60	加	KA, *kuwa(eru/waru)* **add, increase.** *STRENGTH* 𠂔 *"added" to one's speech (* ⼝ *MOUTH):* 加 .
61	売 ⁷	BAI, *u(ru)* **sell.** *Originally:* 賣 . *To take out (* 屮 *new shoots* 屮 *coming out from the mother-plant* ⼃ *) something of value (* 貝 *SHELL, formerly used as money) from a shopping net* 网 *in order to sell it:* 賣 .
62	利	RI **profit, interest, advantage.** *The GRAIN* 禾 *has been cut* 刂 *(KNIFE):* 利 .
63	値 ¹⁰	CHI, *ne* **price;** *atai* **value, price.** Phonogram: [Chih²] = Rad. + 直 Chih² (Ph.842).
64	商 ¹¹	SHO, *akina(u)* **trade/deal in.** *When WORDS* 言 *are spoken inside* 內 *(an object ENTER* 入 *a certain space* ⼌ *) a room, lasting* **several days (** ☉☉ SUNs): 商 .

65	買 [12]	BAI, *ka(u)* **buy.** *To put something of value (貝 SHELL, formerly used as money) in a shopping net 罒 -- after it has been bought:* 買 .
66	貿	BŌ **trade, exchange.** *DOOR 門 that is open 卯 and money (貝 SHELL) formerly used as money) passing through it:* 貿 .
67	貸	TAI, *ka(su/shi)* **lend, rent.** Phonogram: [Tai⁴] = Rad. + 代 Tai⁴ (Ph.329).
68	業 [13]	GYŌ **business, industry.** *A TREE 木 crowned with its foliage 丵 symbolizing a person's activity and its outcome:* 業 .

FOOD

69	米 6	MAI, *kome* **rice (uncooked)**: BEI **America.** *Four grains of rice, scattered ⟩⟨ due to thrashing* 十 : 米 ·
70	肉	NIKU **meat, flesh.** *Strips of dried meat, bundled together:* (大) ·
71	卵 7	RAN, *tamago* **egg.** *Representing the ovaries and oviduct of a female:* ⊕⊕ ·
72	茶 9	CHA, SA **tea.** ψ *The tree-like (木 TREE) plant (ΨΨ GRASS) that* *gives joy (joyful drink) to mankind (𝝠 MAN) :* ·
73	食	SHOKU **food;** *ta(beru)* **eat.** *A pot with contents ⊟ , a ladle ⟨, and the symbol △* *(three lines coming together) to suggest mixing:* ·
74	酒 10	SHU, *sake* **liquor; saké, rice wine.** *WINE JUG 酉 and its contents 氵 (see WATER,* *liquid):* 氵酉 ·
75	飯 12	HAN, *meshi* **rice (cooked).** Phonogram: [Fan⁴] = Rad. + 反 Fan² (Ph.215).

11

GOOD LUCK SIGNS

76 平 ⁵	HEI, BYŌ, *tai(ra na), hira(tai)* **even, level.** *The breath ⸍ going through an obstacle and spreading out evenly 兀 : 丂.*
77 吉 ⁶	KICHI, KITSU **good fortune.** *Good fortune as fortold (ㅂ MOUTH) by a sage (± SCHOLAR): 吉.*
78 寿 ⁷	JU, *kotobuki* **longevity.** *Originally: 壽. Praying for long life (ㅂ MOUTH; ⸜ HAND making gestures stressing request); [HAIR ⸜ that has changed (MAN 人 MAN-upside-down ⸍, i.e. that has changed his position) and wrinkles(畐 furrow)]: 壽.*
79 祥 ¹⁰	SHŌ **good fortune, omen.** Phonogram: [Hsiang²] = Rad. + 羊 *Yang²* (Ph.151).
80 運 ¹²	UN **luck, fortune;** *hako(bu)* **transport.** Phonogram: [Yun⁴] = Rad. + 軍 *Chun¹* (Ph.838).
81 喜	KI, *yoroko(basu/bu/bi)* **delight, (joy)ful.** *There is music (a HAND ⸜ holding a stick — beating a drum-on-a-stand 豆) and singing (ㅂ MOUTH): 喜.*
82 善	ZEN, *i(i), yo(i)* **good.** *Dispute (誩 WORDs) peacefully (羊 SHEEP) settled and harmony restored: 善.*

83	楽 [13]	GAKU **music;** RAKU **comfort.** *Originally:* 樂 . *A musical instrument: a frame with a drum (in the middle) and bells (on the side):* 樂 .
84	福	FUKU **good fortune, wealth.** Phonogram: [Fu²] = Rad. + 畐 Fu² (Ph.816).
85	愛	AI, *ai(suru)* **love.** *To swallow* 旡 *[person く (see MAN) breathing in air* 川 *] affectionate feelings down in one's HEART* 心 *. The symbol* 夊 *means: it is a lingering feeling (a person* 刀 *(see MAN) who slowly advances in spite of an obstacle* ~ *):*

HUMAN BODY

86	力 ²	RYOKU, RIKI, *chikara* **strength, power.** *Picture of a muscle in its sheath:* 𛰄 .
87	口 ³	KŌ, KU, *kuchi* **mouth.** *Picture of the mouth:* ∪
88	心 ⁴	SHIN, *kokoro* **heart, spirit.** *Picture of the heart: the sac* ⌣ *opened; the lobes and the aorta* ⏝ *are also seen:* ⏝.
89	手	SHU, *te* **hand.** *Picture of the hand with the five fingers clearly shown:* ✍ .
90	毛	MŌ, *ke* **hair.** *Picture of a bundle of hair :* ψ .
91	目 ⁵	MOKU, BOKU, *me* **eye;** *-me* **ordinal suffix.** *Picture of an eye* ◯ *, set upright* 𐑫 *in order to take up minimum space.*
92	皮	HI, *kawa* **skin, leather.** *The skin* ? *stripped off by a hand* 𐑦 *holding a knife* ⊃ : 皮.
93	耳 ⁶	JI, *mimi* **ear.** *Picture of the ear:* 耳 .

94	舌	ZETSU, *shita* **tongue.** *The tongue ∀ shown outside the mouth ⊟ : 𝌡 .*
95	足 7	SOKU, *ashi* **foot, leg** *The foot ⊥, with the ankle, heel and toes at rest ○ : 𝌡 . (cp. PROCEED 辵).*
96	身	SHIN, *mi* **body.** *A person, shown with a conpicuous abdomen: 𝌡 .*
97	面 9	MEN **face, surface, mask.** *The face ⬭ with the nose 𝌡 in the center: 𝌡 .*
98	胃	I **stomach.** *Pepresenting the stomach ⊗ containing food ∴ ; and 𝌡 FLESH, the Radical: 𝌡 .*
99	骨 10	KOTSU, *hone* **bone.** *Picture of a human skeleton: 𝌡 .*
100	眼 11	GAN, GEN, *manako, me* **eye.** Phonogram: [Yen³] = Rad. + 艮 *Ken⁴* (Ph.359).
101	鼻 14	BI, *hana* **nose.** *The nose 𝌡 on the human body (represented by 畀 − body ⊕ on legs 丌): 𝌡 .*
102	頭 16	TŌ, TO, ZU, *atama, kashira* **head, top.** Phonogram:[Tou²]= Rad.+ 豆 Tou⁴ (Ph.731).

103	市 5	SHI **city;** *ichi* **market.** *An open space*)—⟨ *grown with grass* Ψ *where one obtains* ⟨ *one's necessities:* 𰀀 .
104	会 6	KAI **meeting, society.** *Originally:* 會 . *A meeting (△ three lines coming together) where words* 𐐠 *(see SPEAK) are spoken at the fireside (⟅⟆ smoke outlet)* 𝌀
105	局 7	KYOKU **bureau, office.** *A place where people work: where words (* 𐐠 *MOUTH) and hands (* 𝌀 *span of a hand*) *are used:* 𝌀 .
106	町	CHŌ, *machi* **town.** Phonogram: [T'ing³] = Rad. + 丁 Ting¹ (Ph.2).
107	京 8	KYŌ, KEI **capital, metropolis.** *Picture of the capital's tower:* 𝌀 .
108	国	KOKU, *kuni* **country.** *Originally* 國 . *A country* ⬭ *with its capital* ○ *that is defended by weapons* 𝌀 *(HALBERD):* 𝌀
109	所	SHO, *tokoro* **place.** Phonogram: [So³] = Rad. + 戶 *Hu⁴* (Ph.728) .

110	官	**KAN government; official, officer.** *The government represented by the capital, namely a building* ⌂ *(DWELLING) with many steps* 𠂤 : 官
111	校 [10]	**KŌ school, correction.** Phonogram: [Hsiao⁴] = Rad. + 交 *Chiao¹* (Ph.531).
112	華 [11]	**KA, KE, *hana* flower; China.** *Leaves and flowers on a branch* 𣎳 *that are expanding* 𠦜 *(breath* ⼃ *expanding freely* — *after passing through an obstacle* ⼀ *) into full bloom :* 華 .
113	都	**TO, TSU, *miyako* capital, metropolis.** Phonogram: [Tu¹] = Rad. + 者 *Chê³* (Ph. 192).
114	街 [12]	**GAI, KAI, *machi* street.** *FOOTSTEPS* 彳亍 *(see GO) and part of the land* 圭 *[* 土 *EARTH (2x)] on which people walk:* 街
115	港	**KŌ, *minato* harbor.** Phonogram: [Kang³] = Rad. + 巷 *Hsiang⁴* (Ph.96).
116	場	**JŌ, *ba* place.** Phonogram: [Ch'ang⁴] = Rad. + 昜 *Yang²* (Ph.236).

17

LOCATIONS

117	上 3	JŌ, SHŌ, *ue* **top;** *a(geru/garu)* *An object* ｜ *above a certain level* 丄 .
118	下	KA, GE, *shita* **bottom;** *sa(geru/garu)* **lower.** *An object* ｜ *below a certain level* 丅 .
119	内 4	NAI, *uchi* **inside.** *To ENTER* 人 *into a certain space* 冂 *:* 内.
120	区	KU **division, ward (sector in a town).** *Originally:* 區 . *To put things (* 口 *MOUTH to represent an object)* *inside a BOX* 匚 *:* 區 *. [Orig. meaning: " lodging",* *etc.]*
121	中	CHŪ, *naka* **middle, inside;** *-jū* **throughout.** *A target*)—(*pierced in the center by an arrow* ｜ *:*)┼(.
122	北 5	HOKU, *kita* **north.** *Two people* 𠤎 *(see MAN) turning their backs to* *the North* 𠤎 *. (Facing the South was a custom* *during ceremonies; the Emperor living in the* *North of his country, faced the South to look* *over his domain.):* 𠤎 .
123	央	Ō **center, middle.** *A person* 大 *in the center of space* ├┤ *:* 央.

124	**GE**, *soto* **outside; GAI foreign.** *DIVINATION* ⌐ *done in the evening* ☽ *, i.e.* *'outside' the normal hours, because divination* *must be done immediately after the dream, that is* *before the evening comes:* ☽⌐ *.*
125	**SA**, *hidari* **left.** *The left hand ⦰ , the one that holds the carpenter's* *square* ⼯ *:* ⦰ .
126	**YŪ, U**, *migi* **right.** *The right HAND* ⼚ *: the one that is used when* *eating (* ⼝ *MOUTH):* ⼚ .
127	**CHI, JI** **earth, ground.** *Phonogram:* [Ti⁴] = Rad. + 也 *Yeh³ (Ph.301).*
128	**SEI, SAI**, *nishi* **west.** *Originally:* 圙 . *When birds* ⼕ *sit on their nests* ⼕ *, it is evening* *and the sun is in the west.*
129	**TŌ**, *higashi* **east.** *The SUN* ☉ *is in the East when it is so low that* *one can see it behind the TREE* ⽊ *(of the East-* *ern mountains):* ⽊ .
130	**GO**, *nochi* **after (wards); KŌ**, *ushi(ro)* **back,** **behind.** *To march (FOOTSTEP* ⼷ *; PURSUE* ⼡ *),* *while leaving a trail by stretching out a THREAD* ⼂ *behind:* ⼷⼂ .

131	南	NAN, NA, *minami* **south.** *The area⟩ ⟨where vegetation (ψ plant) expands continuously (⊻ PESTLE); the additional stroke suggests the idea of repetition or continuity:* ⟩⊻⟨ .
132	前	ZEN, *mae* **before, in front of, previous.** *A BOAT 舟 that STOPs ⊔ in front of the harbor:* 俞 .

133	不 [4]	FU, BU **(neg. pref.), not, un-.** *An upward flying bird with wings backwards* 朩 *trying in vain to reach the sky* — : 朩 .
134	田 [5]	DEN, *ta* **rice field.** *Picture of a field with furrows:* ⊕ .
135	台	DAI **a stand, platform.** *Originally:* 臺 . *Representing a mound of earth, used as a look-out platform:* 茎 .
136	字 [6]	JI **character, letter.** *A child* 子 *carefully reared in the house* ⌂ *(DWELLING):* 字 . *By extension: a* **Kanji character** , *because it is the result of careful mixing of writing-units.*
137	空 [8]	KŪ, *sora* **sky;** *a(keru/ku)* **empty.** *Phonogram:* [K'ung³] = Rad. + 工 Kung¹ (Ph. 8).
138	香 [9]	KŌ **incense** KYŌ, *kaori* **fragrance, smell.** *The SWEET* ⊌ *odor of fermented (* ∧ *vapors) GRAIN* 禾 : 香 .
139	是	ZE **right, just.** *The SUN* ⊖ *seems to STOP* 止 *right above the equator* — : 是 .
140	真 [10]	SHIN, *ma* **truth.** *TEN + EYEs* ⊖ *looking at something put on a pedestal* 兀 *and finding nothing wrong (* ∟ *straight angle):* 眞 .

141	特	TOKU **special.** Phonogram: [T'e⁴] = Rad. + 寺 *Ssû⁴* (Ph.46).
142	郵 ¹¹	YŪ **post, mail.** Phonogram: [Yu²] = Rad. + 垂 *Ch'ui²* (Ph. 26).
143	語 ¹⁴	GO **word, language.** *Originally:* 語 . Phonogram: [Yü³] = Rad. + 吾 *Wu²* (Ph.763).

144	川 [3]	SEN, *kawa* **river.** *A big stream formed by smaller streams:* 川 .
145	山	SAN, *yama* **mountain.** *Picture of a mountain* 山 .
146	土	DO, TO, *tsuchi* **earth, ground.** *The layer* 二 *from which all things* 丨 *came out:* 土 .
147	火 [4]	KA, *hi* **fire, flame.** *A pile of wood burning with flames* 火 .
148	水	SUI, *mizu* **water.** *A stream* 丨 *with whirls of water* 川 : 水 .
149	日	NICHI, JITSU, *hi* **day, sun;** *-ka* **number of days.** *Picture of the sun:* 日 .
150	天	TEN, *ame* **heaven, sky.** *That which expands* 一 *over mankind* 大 *(see BIG):* 天 .
151	月	GETSU, *tsuki* **moon, month.** *Picture of a crescent moon:* 月 .
152	石 [5]	SEKI, SHAKU, *ishi* **stone.** *Showing a stone* ○ *in a cliff* 厂 : 石 .

153	氷	HYŌ, *kōri, hi* **ice.** *WATER* 川 *that has crystallized (* 冫 *crystals):* 氷 .
154	世	SE, SEI, *yo* **world.** *Three TEN's* 十 *combined:* 卋, *i.e. "thirty", which was the average age of a person in ancient times. [Orig. meaning: "generation".]*
155	光 ⁶	KŌ, *hika(ru)* **light, ray.** *FIRE* 火 *carried by a person* 儿 *(MAN):* 光 .
156	金 ⁸	KIN, KON **gold;** *kane* **money.** *Four nuggets (ore)* 𤆍 *burried (* 亼 *cover) in the EARTH* 土 : 金 .
157	岩	GAN, *iwa* **rock, crag.** *A rock* 石 *(STONE) coming from a MOUNTAIN* 山 : 岩 .
158	雨	U, *ame* **rain.** *Drops of water* == *falling down* 丨 *from clouds* ⌒ *suspended from the sky* 一 : 雨 .
159	河	KA, *kawa* **river.** *Phonogram: [Ho²] = Rad. +* 可 *K'o²* (Ph.699).
160	泉 ⁹	SEN, *izumi* **spring (fountain).** *WATER* 川 *spouting up* 丶 *and expanding evenly* 几 泉 .

161	海	KAI, *umi* **sea.** *The mother 毎 (WOMAN 女 with breasts ／ヽadded)* *of all (Ψ grass, to suggests "omnipresence")* *WATER 氵 . 灥 .*
162	界	KAI **border, boundary; world.** Phonogram: [Chieh⁴] = Rad. + 介 Chieh⁴ (Ph.433).
163	星	SEI, SHŌ, *hoshi* **star.** *Sublimated matter ascending ∪ from the EARTH* *土, to become stars ○○ : 望 .*
164	風	FŪ, FU, *kaze* **wind; style.** *Motion of air 几 and an insect 虫 . (It was be-* *lieved that insects were born when the wind* *blew.): 風 .*
165	洋	YŌ **ocean; western.** Phonogram: [Yang²] = Rad. + 羊 Yang² (Ph.151).
166	島 ¹⁰	TŌ, *shima* **island.** *A MOUNTAIN 山 in the sea on which BIRDs 鳥* *can rest while crossing: 島 .*
167	雪 ¹¹	SETSU, *yuki* **snow.** *RAIN 雨 that has solidified into snow, and held in* *one's HAND ⺕ : 雪 .*
168	湖 ¹²	KO, *mizuumi* **lake.** Phonogram: [Hu²] = Rad. + 胡 Hu² (Ph.705).

169	雲	UN, *kumo* **cloud.** *Vapors ⌒ of water that rise to the sky─and will later come down as RAIN* 雨 *:* 雲 *.*
170	電 [13]	DEN **lightning, electricity.** *That which extends ∖∃ from the RAIN* 雨 *and strikes down* ∖ *:* 電 *.*
171	銀 [14]	GIN **silver.** *No. 156* *Metal* 金 *(see GOLD) and* 艮 *DEFIANCE, suggesting that silver is malleable ('defies' the action of a hammer):* 銀 *.*

NUMBERS

172	一	*ichi* **one.** *One stroke, to represent the number 'one':* 一 .
173	二	NI, *futa* **two.** *Two strokes, representing the number 'two':* 二 .
174	三	SAN, *mit(tsu), mitsu-* **three** *Three strokes:* 三 .
175	四	SHI, *yo-, yon-* **four.** *A quantity that can be divided into two equal* *portions:* ⑪ .
176	五	GO, *itsu(tsu), itsu-* **five.** *Symbol for a unit* ✕ : *as used in the abacus – we* *have five fingers on each hand.*
177	六	ROKU, *mut(tsu), mu(tsu)* **six.** *A quantity that can be divided into two equal* *portions (with a dot • added to distinguish it from* **four** ⑪): ⑫ .
178	七	SHICHI, *nana(tsu), nana-* **seven.** *Symbol for a unit used in fortune telling (with* *a 'tail' to distinguish it for unit "ten"* ✛ : ✚ .
179	八	HACHI, HATSU, *yat(tsu), ya(tsu), ya-* **eight.** *A quantity consisting of two equal halves:*)(.

180	九	KYŪ, KU, *kokono(tsu), kokono* **nine.** *Almost a unit: a wavy " ten "* 十 : 九 .
181	十	JŪ, *tō* **ten.** *Symbol for a unit:* 十 .
182	百	HYAKU **hundred.** Phonogram: [Pai³] = Rad. + 白 Pai² (Ph.804).
183	千	SEN, *chi* **thousand.** *Ten* 十 *platoons of men (* 人 *MAN), i.e. one thousand men:* 千 .
184	万	MAN **ten thousand.** *Originally:* 萬 . *Picture of a scorpion, with its head* ⊕ *, legs and tail* ᙏ *and its 'thousands' of claws:* 𝄢 : 萬
185	多	TAI, *ō(i)* **many.** *Many objects* 夕 *(EVENING, used here to represent 'object', because it is easy to write):* 多 .
186	少	SHŌ, *suko(shi)* **a little, a few.** *What is left after taking away* 乙 *a little from something that is already small:* 小²³² : 少 .
187	双	SŌ, *futa* **two, both, a pair; twin(s).** *Originally:* 雙 . *One HAND* 又 *holding two BIRDs* 隹隹 : 雙 .
188	半	HAN, *naka(ba)* **half.** *An OX* 牛 *split into two equal portions, namely by cutting it lengthwise, the way butchers do:* 半 .

189	号	**GŌ issue/number.** *A statement (breath) coming out — from the* *MOUTH* .
190	毎	**MAI every.** *Grass Ψ , which can be found everwhere; and* **mother** * ,*which gives the idea of fertility:* . * (See in SEA No. 161.)
191	共	**KYŌ, tomo together.** *Twenty (two TENs + +connected) HANDs* *joined together in a joined effort:* .
192	隻	**SEKI unit for counting ships.** *A HAND holding one BIRD* : .
193	第	**DAI rank.** *A thread being wound around a BAMBOO* *spool , giving the idea of succession:* .
194	幾	**KI, iku(tsu) how many/much.** *A guard [MAN with a spear (HALBERD)]* *listening to the slightest (THREAD) movements:* .
195	数	**SŪ, SU, kazu number; kazo(eru) count.** *To watch over (HAND holding stick) women* *prisoners(WOMAN locked in prison):* .

196	刀 ²	TŌ, *katana* **knife; sword.** *Picture of a knife* ∧ *; later the handle was curved upwards for compactness* �𠃌 .
197	皿 ⁵	*sara* **dish.** *Picture of a dish mounted on a pedestal* 𝚷 *, as used during banquets.*
198	玉	GYOKU, *tama* **jewel.** *The precious gem* • *that only kings* 王 *(the mediator* │ *between Heaven* ⁻ *, Earth* ⎵ *and Man* ⁻ *) could possess:* 王̇ .
199	矢	SHI, *ya* **arrow.** *Picture of an arrow* 夨 .
200	衣 ⁶	I, *koromo* **clothing, garment.** *A robe and its sleeves* ∠ *and* ∧ *its dragging over the floor:* 衣 .
201	車 ⁷	SHA, *kuruma* **cart; car; vehicle; wheel.** *A cart seen from above* 車 *, showing the body* ⊕ *, axle* │ *and wheels* ⁼ .
202	杯 ⁸	HAI **cup.** Phonogram: [Pei¹] = Rad. + 不 *Puᴵ* (Ph.120).
203	画	GA, KAKU **picture.** *Originally:* 畫 . *A HAND* ⇒ *holding a stylus* │ *drawing a line* ⁻ *on a drawing board* ∧ *, and* 𝑓卣 *[the resulting drawing* ⊕ *put in a frame* 凵 *]:* 畫 .

204	服	FUKU **dress/clothes; dose; obey.** *Etymology ?*
205	物	*mono* **thing, object.** Phonogram: [Wu⁴] = Rad. + 勿 Wu⁴ (Ph.233).
206	表	HYŌ, *omote* **table, chart; surface.** *Representing the outside of a fur coat (CLOTHES) with the hair (HAIR), which revealed the function of the imperial huntsman: [Orig. meaning: "the outside of a garment".]*
207	宝	HO, *takara* **treasure.** *Originally:* 寶 . *Treasure in one's house (DWELLING), represented by JADE 王(three pieces of jade on a string), porcelain (EARTHENWARE) and money (SHELL formerly used as money):*
208	9 計	KEI – **meter (as suffix);** *haka(ru)* **gauge, measure.** *To be able to pronounce (WORDS) the numbers ONE (一) to TEN (十), which was the minimal requirement if one wanted to do some calculation. (Orig. meaning: "to calculate", etc.):*
209	10 紙	SHI, *kami* **paper.** Phonogram: [Chih³] = Rad. + 氏 Shih⁴ (Ph.348).

210	席	SEKI **seat, place.** *Mats (/⺁CLOTH) upon which guests sat during ancient times' banquets [⌠¯ SHELTER (house); ⼞ = ++ = two TENs = many (guests)]:* .
211	筆 12	HITSU, *fude* **writing brush.** *A BAMBOO⺮ writing brush (a HAND ⇒ holding a stylus | drawing a line — on a tablet ⼈):* .

PERSONS

212	人 ²	JIN, NIN, *hito* **person.** *That being who is standing on two legs:* ∬.⊓.⅄.
213	子 ³	SHI, *ko* **child.** *A newborn child with the legs still bound in swathes* Ϙ.
214	女	JO, NYŌ, *onna* **woman; female.** *Picture of a woman:* 久.
215	父 ⁴	FU, *chichi* **father.** *A hand* ⅃ *holding a rod* ∣, *to express authority:* Ϩ.
216	友	YŪ, *tomo* **friend.** *Two HANDs working in the same direction:* ⅀.
217	夫	FU, FŪ, *otto* **husband.** *An adult MAN* 火 *with a pin* — *in his hair: token of maturity:* 夰.
218	王	Ō **king.** *The mediator* ∣ *between Heaven* ⌐, *Earth* __ *and* — *Man* 王.
219	氏	SHI **Mr. ; family, clan.** *Representing a floating plant* Ψ *that multiplies itself and grows in abundance:* Ɛ.

220	公	KŌ, ōyake **public.** *Division*)(*and distribution of a private posses-* *sion (* δ *cocoon; with the self-enclosed silkworm* *it gives the idea of privacy):*)δ(.
221	母 [5]	BO, haha **mother.** *A WOMAN* ⊗ *with breasts*)(*added to distin-* *guished her from a WOMAN* ⊗ *who has not* *become a mother yet.*
222	民	MIN, tami **people.** *Weed that grows in abundance (* ⅄ *and* 𝒏 *are* *the small stems and leaves):* 𝕏 .
223	自 [6]	JI, SHI, mizuka(ra) **oneself, in person.** *Picture of a NOSE:* 自 .
224	后	KŌ **empress, queen.** *A person* 𝒏 *(MAN) bending over* Γ *giving* *orders (* ⊔ *MOUTH) to people:* 后 .
225	医 [7]	I **doctor(medical).** *Originally:* 醫 . *Taking out* 殳 *(HAND* ヲ *making jerky motion* ⌒) *ARROW* 矢 *from receptacle* 匚 , *in order to shoot* *down the demon; and to give elixir (* 酋 *WINE JUG)* *to the patient:* 醫 .
226	私	SHI, watakushi **I.** Phonogram: [Szu[1]] = Rad. + ㄙ Ssŭ (Ph.868).

227	男	DAN, NAN, *otoko* **man.** *The one that gives his STRENGTH 力 in the* *FIELD ⊕. (The woman doing her work inside the* *house.):* 男.
228	君	KUN **(fam. suf.) Mr.;** *kimi* **(fam.) you.** *Originally:* 君. *A HAND 크 holding a scepter ⎸, and a MOUTH* *ㅂ that gives orders to people.*
229	妻 [8]	SAI **my wife;** *tsuma* **wife.** *The WOMAN 女 who holds (크 HAND) a duster Ψ :* 妻 .
230	皇 [9]	KŌ, Ō **emperor.** Phonogram: [Huang²] = Rad. + 王 Wang² (Ph.71).

231	大 ³	DAI, TAI, ō(kii), ō(ki na) **big, great.** *A man with outstretched arms as if showing the size of large object:* 大 .
232	小	SHŌ, chii(sai), ko-, o- **small.** *An object*) \ *split*	*into two:* 川 . *****
233	太 ⁴	TAI, TA, futo(i) **big, thick.** *Same as No.1, with a dot ▪ added:* 太 .
234	巨 ⁵	KYO **huge, gigantic; giant.** *A large carpenter's square* 工 *which has a handle* コ: 巨 .
235	長 ⁸	CHŌ **head, leader;** naga(i) **long.** *Hair* ⼕ *so long that it is tied with a band* ─ *and a brooch* ⼃ : 長 .
236	厚 ⁹	KŌ, atsu(i) **thick, cordial.** *Generosity expressed by a gift* ⊖ *coming down* ⼂ *from above (* ⼦ *gift received):* 厚 .
237	高 ¹⁰	KŌ, taka(i) **high, expensive.** *Picture of a tower:* 高 .
238	短 ¹²	TAN, mijika(i) **short.** *A dart* 矢 *(small arrow) and a platter-on-a-pedestal* 豆 , *i.e. two short utensils:* 矢豆

* Other explanation: *A person with arms put together as if showing the size of a small object :* 小 .

239	又 [2]	*mata* **again.** *The right HAND 肀 rather than the left hand 屮 being used most of the time, it is used 'again and again'.*
240	久 [3]	KYŪ, KU, *hisa(shii)* **long(time).** *A person 乃 (see MAN) while walking is meeting an obtruction ヽ: 久.*
241	夕	SEKI, *yū* **evening.** *A wavy half-moon, just appearing above the horizon: ⊃.*
242	分 [4]	FUN **minute;** BUN **share, lot;** *wa(keru)* **divide.** *A KNIFE 勹 divides an object into two small portions 八: 州.*
243	今	KON, *ima* **now.** *The time that follows ⌐ the past (the time that has come full circle: three lines that come together △):今 .*
244	午	GO **noon.** *Picture of an ancient sundial to mark the noontime: 中.*
245	月	GETSU, *tsuki* **moon, month.** *Picture of a crescent moon: 刀 .*
246	冬 [5]	TŌ, *fuyu* **winter.** *The end 夊 (the knot at the end of a sewing thread) of the year when ice 仌 (ice crystals) appear: 冬.*

247	永	EI, *naga(i)* **long time, lasting.** *Representing veins of water in the Earth flowing incessantly:* 氷.
248	古	KO, *furu(i)* **old.** *When it has passed from MOUTH* 廿 *to mouth over many (* 十 *TEN) generations:* 古 .
249	未	MI **not yet.** *A TREE* 木 *not yet fully grown, i.e. the top portion* ∪ *is not fully developed:* 朱 .
250	年 [6]	NEN, *toshi* **year.** *The time it takes to harvest all (* 千 **thousand**, No. 183) *the GRAIN* 禾 .
251	早	SŌ, *haya(i)* **morning; early, fast.** *When the SUN* ⊖ *has risen to the height of a soldier's helmet* 宁 : 㫃
252	再	SAI, SA, *futata(bi)* **again.** *Representing a second* = *(TWO) weighing on a weighing scale* 丙 : 再 .
253	先	SEN, *saki* **prior, previous, future.** *To advance* 丄 *(a plant* Ψ *coming out from the ground* 一 *) with one's feet* 儿 : 先 .
254	次	JI, SHI, *tsugi(no)* **next.** *Taking breath* 欠 *(see BREATHE) one after another* (= *TWO) :* 次.
255	即 [7]	SOKU **immediate(ly).** *Soup* 皀 (㓁 *a pot and* 匕 *a spoon) and a soup ladle, i.e. soup that can be immediately served:* 即 .

256	夜 8	YA, *yoru, yo* **night.** *When a person* 大 *(see BIG) is turning aside* ノ *in order to sleep in the EVENING* ⼣ : 夜 .
257	春 9	SHUN, *haru* **spring.** *The SUN* ⊖ *and the sprouting of plants* 屮屮 *(*屮屮 *plants):* 萅 .
258	昨	SAKU **yester-, the past.** Phonogram: [Tso²] = Rad. + 乍 *Cha⁴* (Ph.150).
259	秋	SHŪ, *aki* **autumn.** *When the GRAIN* 禾 *in the field ripens and attains a fiery* 火 *(FIRE) color:* 秌 .
260	昼	CHŪ, *hiru* **noon, daytime.** *Originally:* 晝 . *Time limit* ⼞ *during which it is light (* ⊖ *SUN) enough for people to write* 聿 *: (see STYLUS):* 晝
261	時 10	JI, *toki* **time.** *The SUN* ⊖ *and to measure [i.e. 'to measure the pulse'* 寸 *(place on the HAND* 寸 *indicated by the dash* - *) the growth of plants* 㞢 *:* 旹 .
262	夏	KA, GE, *natsu* **summer.** *A person [represented only by the nose* 自 *(see NOSE)] with idle hands* 臼 *walking at leisure* 夂 *(see PURSUE):* 夏 .

263	週 [11]	SHŪ **week.** Phonogram: [Chou¹] = Rad. + 周 Chou¹ (Ph.730).
264	朝 [12]	CHŌ, *asa* **morning.** *The rising 屮 SUN ☉ as seen from a BOAT 月* *through the jungle (mangrove tree with its* *branches hanging down striking roots):* .
265	晚	BAN **evening.** Phonogram: [Wan³] = Rad. + 免 *Mien²* (Ph.384).
266	歲 [13]	SEI **year;** SAI **year, year old.** *Originally:* 歲 . Phonogram: [Sui⁴] = Rad. + 戌 *Hsü¹* (Ph.342).

TRAVEL

267	出 ⁵	SHUTSU, SUI, *da(su)* **go out, put out.** *New shoots* 𝒰 *coming out from the mother-plant* 𐤀 : 𝒰.
268	至 ⁶	SHI **extreme;** *ita(ru)* **arrive (at).** *A bird with wings backward* 𝜓 *coming down and reaching the EARTH* 土: 𝜓.
269	行	KŌ, AN, *i(ku)*, *yu(ku)* **go.** *Footsteps made by left and right feet:* 彳川.
270	舟	SHŪ, *fune* **boat.** *A hollowed tree trunk* 月 (片 *represents half of a TREE* 米), *representing a BOAT.*
271	到 ⁸	TŌ **reach, arrive at.** *A bird with wings backwards* 𝜓 *flying down and reaching the EARTH* 土: 𝜓刂. (刂 = Ph. 219).
272	飛 ⁹	HI, *to(bu)* **fly.** *Picture of a flying crane:* 飛.
273	旅 ¹⁰	RYO, *tabi* **journey.** *Men* 从 *(see* 人 *MAN) on a journey, finding shelter during bad weather under the overhanging branches* 𐀀 *of a tree* 𝒴 *(see* 米 *TREE):* 旅.
274	航	KŌ **navigation, voyage.** *A BOAT* 舟 *and the navigator resolutely standing* 𐅂 *on both legs:* 舟亢.

船 11	SEN, *fune* **ship.** *A BOAT* 舟 *cleaving* ノ \ *the surface* ⊔ *of the* *water:* 船 .
遊 12	YŪ, YU, *aso(bu)* **play, enjoy oneself.** *PROCEED* 辵 *and* 斿 *(person with arms making* *fluttering motions, swimming aimlesly) and* 孚 * (see CHILD):* 遊 .

* The symbol 孚 (CHILD, with the legs bound in swathes) suggests that the persons legs are not visible because they are under the water.

277	木 ⁴	**MOKU, BOKU,** *ki* **tree, wood.** *Picture of a tree, showing the trunk* | *, with the branches* ⌄ *and the roots* ⌒ : 米.
278	本 ⁵	**HON, book;** *moto* **source, origin.** *Orig. meaning: the roots (the bottom part* ― *) of a* TREE 米 : 本.
279	瓜	**KA,** *uri* **melon.** *Picture of the melon plant and its fruit:* 瓜.
280	竹 ⁶	**CHIKU,** *take* **bamboo.** *Picture of BAMBOO trees with drooping leaves* 个个.
281	豆 ⁷	**TŌ, ZU,** mame **beans, peas.** *A simple meal of BEANs • on a stemmed platter:* 豆.
282	花 ⁸	**KA,** *hana* **flower.** *The portion of plants* 屮屮 *that has greatly changed* 化 *[a person* 乃 *(MAN) and* 匕 *person-upside-down, i.e. a person who has "changed" position]:* 花.
283	果	**KA,** *hata(su)* **fruit.** *A fruit* ⊕ *that grows on a TREE* 米 : 果.
284	林	**RIN,** *hayashi* **wood, grove.** *Where many TREEs* 米 *are growing:* 林米.
285	薬 ¹¹	**YAKU,** *kusuri* **medicine.** *Originally:* 藥. Phonogram: [Yao⁴] = Rad. + 樂 *Lo⁴* (Ph.490).

VERBS

286	入 [2]	NYU, *hai(ru)* **enter;** *i(reru)* **put/let in.** *Representing a plant with its roots penetrating the soil:* 人 .
287	引 [4]	IN, *hi(ku/ki)* **pull.** *To pull at the string* | *of a BOW* 弓 : 弓| .
288	止	SHI, *to(meru/maru)* **stop.** *Representing the foot-at-rest, showing the heel* ∟ , *the toe* ⌐ *and the ankle* ⼓ *of a foot:* ⼞ *(see FOOT).*
289	立 [5]	RITSU, *ta(tsu/chi)* **stand.** *A man* 大 *(see BIG) standing on the ground* — : 立 .
290	去	KYO, KO, *sa(ru)* **leave.** *An empty vessel* ⼂ ; *its content has been taken away and its lid* 大 *has been put back:* 去 .
291	包	HŌ, *tsutsu(mu)* **wrap (v).** *Picture of a foetus "wrapped" in the womb:* 包 .
292	加	KA, *kuwa(eru/waru)* **add, increase.** *STRENGTH* 力 *"added" to one's speech (* 口 *MOUTH):* 加 .
293	休 [6]	KYŪ, *yasu(mu/mi)* **rest, repose.** *A person* 亻 *(MAN) resting under a TREE* 木 : 休 .

294	回	KAI **turn, time**; *mawa(su/ru)* **turn.** *Representing a whirlpool, where the water turns round rapidly:* ⊚ .
295	走 [7]	SŌ, *hashi(ru)* **run.** *A man with his head bent downward* 夭 *who runs* (止 *foot, see STOP) quickly:* 쥿 .
296	言	*i(u)/yu(u)* **say**; GEN, GON, *-koto-* **word.** *The TONGUE* 설 *and words* (═ *sound waves) being produced by it:* 哲 *(WORDS).*
297	来	RAI, *ku(ru)* **come.** *Originally:* 來 . *A person* 大 *(see BIG) coming down the road with ears of corn* ʌʌ *hanging over the shoulders:* 桼 .
298	見	KEN, *mi(ru)* **see**; *mi(seru)* **show.** *The EYE* 目 *of a person (a being standing on two LEGS* 儿 *):* 見 .
299	完	KAN **complete.** *Putting head gear* ═ *on a person* 氼 *(see MAN) completes a person's dressing. Putting a roof on a house* 宀 *(DWELLING) completes the house:* 완 .
300	歩 [8]	HO, BU, FU, *aru(ku)*, *ayu(mu)* **walk.** *To go "step by step", namely, to "move"* 屮 *[the mirror image of* 止 *(STOP)] and to "STOP" consecutively:* 歩 .
301	取	SHU, *to(ru)* **take.** *A HAND* 彐 *is holding an EAR* 耳 *:* 㕧 .

302	受	JU, *u(keru)* **receive.** *One hand ⚲ transferring ⌐ an object to another person's HAND* ⇒: 㡱 .
303	知	CHI, *shi(ru)* **aware, know.** *To know how to speak (⊔ MOUTH) with precision (an arrow that hits the mark 矢):* 矢⊔ .
304	押	Ō, *o(su)* **push.** *A HAND* ⚿ *and* ⊕ *to represent a downward motion (| going down from* ⊕ *):* ⚿⊕ .
305	学	GAKU, **learning, study; school;** *Originally:* 學 *-ology (suffix); mana(bu)* **learn.** *The CHILD* 𝓢 *in darkness (⌒ small room) and the two hands* ⊨⇛ *of the master pouring knowledge* × *to the child:* ⊨×⇛ .
306	看⁹	KAN **watch, see.** *The HAND* ⚿ *shading the EYE* ⊖ *in order to see better:* 㼿 .
307	送	SŌ, *oku(ru)* **send.** *To escort (PROCEED* � *) a guest carrying a torch (火 FIRE held by a pair of HANDs* ⚿⚿ *):* 𝅘𝅥𝅯 .
308	書¹⁰	SHO, *ka(ku)* **write.** *Representing a STYLUS* 聿 *and the drawing* ⊕ *made by it:* 書 .
309	起	KI, *o(kiru)* **get up, awake;** *o(kosu/koru).* *Putting one's SELF* 㡱 *in motion* 走 *(RUN):* 起 .

310	問 [11]	MON, *to(u)* **ask about, question.** *To be at the DOOR* 門 *and ask (* 口 *MOUTH) a question:* 問 .
311	閉	HEI, *to(jiru), shi(maru/meru)* **shut, close.** *The DOOR* 門 *with the bars* 才 *behind it:* 閉 .
312	開 [12]	KAI, *hira(keru/ku), a(keru/ku)* **open(v).** *A pair of HANDs* 廾 *removing the bar* — *from the DOOR* 門 : 開 .
313	飲	IN, *no(mu)* **drink.** Phonogram: [Yin³] = Rad. + 欠 *Ch'ien⁴* (Ph.441).
314	禁 [13]	KIN, *kin(jiru)* **prohibit.** 示 *Bad omen (see REVELATION) from TREEs* 林 : 禁 .
315	需 [14]	JU **request, need, require; demand.** *A plant requires RAIN* 雨 *in order to develop in full [* 而 *is short for* 耑 : *a plant that develops under and above the ground]:* 需 .

NOTE: There should be only 313 characters, and not 315, because the character 月 occurs two times: in NATURE as **Moon**, and in TIME as **Month**; and the character 加 occurs also two times: in ENTERPRISE and VERBS: as **To add.**

Appendix

How to Write a Kanji Character and Count the Number of Strokes

Writing a Kanji character can be done with a writing-brush or with a pen. When you write with a brush, you are actually creating a work of art. It requires long training and you have to follow strict rules.

Below gives you an idea what rules you are following when you write the character 永 for "long time".

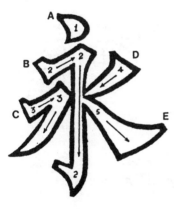

It looks as if this character consists of many strokes, but it actually has only *five*. This is because **B** is one stroke only, and so is **C**. In both cases the writing brush manages to make the "hook" in one continuous movement without lifting it from the paper.

The writing-unit **A** is a "dot". To write **A**, the brush must *make a "twisting" motion.* Unit **B** and **C** are "hooks" are written with one stroke* only. To write **D**, you must write *from right to left, and start by pressing the brush against the paper.* To write **E**, you must write *from left to right and end by pressing the brush against the paper.*

> * A "stroke" *is produced by the brush in one contin-uous movement without lifting it from the paper.*
> A "hook" *counts for "one stroke".*

Fortunately, when writing with a pen you do not have to follow rules. For example, the direction of writing is not important, because you are only drawing *"lines"*. On the other hand, when writing with a brush, you are drawing *"pictures"*, and you must not only know how to manipulate the brush, but also know the direction of writing (see example on previous page).

There is one rule, however, that the pen and the brush have in common when writing a character. In both cases, a *"hook"* is written with one stroke, as shown on the previous page.

With a pen, can you write the characters below?

女	日	金	園	福	愛
Woman	Sun	Gold	Garden	Good luck	Love

The following diagrams give you the solutions.

Numbers at the top-right corners are the number of strokes written so far. Asterisks (*) are placed at "hooks".

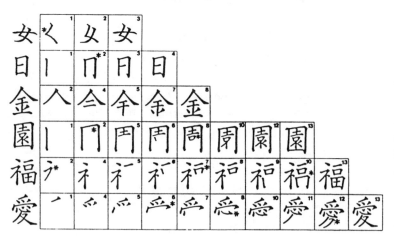

Knowing the number of strokes of a character allows you to locate a character in the Dictionary through the Character Finder (pages A to G at the end of the Appendix), in which *all characters are arranged by the number of their strokes.*

The Dictionary contains complete information about a character, i.e. its pronunciation(s), meaning(s) and etymology (historical explanation).

List of Radicals

The first Kanji characters were pictures or combination of pictures from which their meanings could be derived. Using a stylus they were scratched on bones, wood, etc. They are called **Pictograms** (*picto* = picture; *gram* = writing).

The writing brush replaced the stylus, because the brush, using ink, could namely write characters much easier and faster by writing them on paper. However, pictures could no longer be made, because unlike the stylus the brush could not make the loops and intricate drawings that the pictures contained. And instead of pictures, a character consisted of rough approximations of the original pictures.

There came a new method of creating characters. A new character was formed by combining two existing pictures. One picture showed *to which group of characters a certain character belonged.* It is called the **Radical** (*radix* = root). The other picture *gave the (Chinese) pronunciation of the character*, and is called the *Phonetic* (*phone* = sound).

As time went by, the pronunciation of the character underwent changes and the *Phonetic was no longer the same as the pronunciation of the character.*

In 鶏 **Chicken** [Chi¹], the Phonetic 奚 *Hsi¹* is no longer the same as the Chinese pronunciation [Chi¹] of the character and *Hsi¹* is *printed in italics.*

What follows is a complete List of the 214 Radicals.* A quarter or 79 of them are used in this book and *in this List they are underlined.* And when they appear in the Dictionary, they are *followed by their names in English, written in capitals,* for example: WATER, MOUTH, etc. Instead of explaining their meanings in the Dictionary itself, you are referred to this **List of Radicals** to find the explanations there.

---

* The 214 Radicals came from the *K'ang-hsi Dictionary,* which is the largest Chinese dictionary, containing over 40,000 characters. Commissioned by Emperor K'ang-hsi (1661-1722), it was completed in 1716. In this dictionary the characters were arranged according to their Radicals

List of Radicals

ARROW 矢

Picture of an arrow 矢 .

AXE 斤

Representing an axe 尸 *and* ⼷ *(a chip of wood):* 斤 .

BACK TO BACK 非

Two identical objects placed opposite each other 非

** BAMBOO 竹 . 𥫗

Picture of bamboo trees with drooping leaves 𣎳 .

BASKET 匚

Picture of a basket ⼐ , *turned aside* 匚 .

BEAN 豆

A simple meal of beans • on a stemmed platter: 豆 .

BEARD 而

What hangs down from the chin: 而 .

BENT 乙 . 乚

The bent shape of a germ 乙 .

* BIG 大 . 奄

A man with outstretched arms as if showing the size of a large object 大 .

* BIRD (1) 鳥

Picture of a bird 鳥 .

* *Understanding Chinese Characters by their Ancestral Forms* , by this Author, deals with characters seen in American Chinatowns and cities.

BIRD (2) 隹

Picture of a short-tailed bird 隹 .

BLACK 黑

Soot ⨉ *deposited by a smoky fire* 炎 *around a vent* ⊕ – 羔 .

BLOOD 血

A stemmed vessel 豆 *containing blood* – : 血 .

BOAT 舟

A hollowed tree trunk 舟 , *representing a boat.*

BODY 身

A person, shown with a conspicuous abdomen 身 .

BONES 骨

Picture of a human skeleton 骨 .

BORDERS 冂

The boundaries of some portion of space 冂 .

BOTH FEET 癶

Picture of both feet of a person or animal: 癶 .

BOW 弓

Picture of a Chinese reflex bow 弓 .

BOX 匚

Picture of a box 凵 *turned sideways to allow other components to be written in* 匚 .

BRANCH 支

Originally 㞢: a hand 㞢 pulling off a branch 个 from a tree.

BREATHE 欠

A man 人 breathing out air 彡 : 欠 .

CALDRON 鬲

Representing an ancient three-legged caldron 鬲 .

* CART 車

A cart (seen from above) 車, showing the body ⊕, axle | , and wheels 二 .

CAT 豸

Representing a cat-like animal 豸 .

CAVE 穴 . 空

A cave ∩ resulting from earth being taken away 八 (by the water): 穴 .

CHILD 子

Picture of a newborn child with the legs still bound in swathes 子 .

CITY 邑 . 阝

The city o and its seal 卪 : 邑 .

CLAN 氏

Representing a floating plant that grows in abundance 氏 .

CLAW 爪 . 爫

Picture of a claw 爪 .

CLIFF 厂

Representing a steep cliff 厂.

* CLOTH 巾

Piece of cloth ∩ for cleaning, hanging down | from the girdle: 巾.

** CLOTHES 衣 . 衤

A robe and its sleeves ⊥ and ∧ its dragging over the floor: 衣.

COCOON 厶

Picture of a cocoon ◌.

COLOR 色

A man ⟨ with a red (color of a seal 巴) face: 色.

COMPARE 比

Two men ⟨ standing next to each other, in order to compare their heights 比.

CORPSE 尸

A sitting person 尸, representing the dead.

COVER 冖

Picture of a cover ∧.

DARK 玄

The thread ⸰ (two cocoons twisted into a thread) being dipped ∧ into the dye, and obtaining a dark color: 玄.

DART 弋

A dart (a small arrow), which attached to a string can be retrieved after it has been thrown to kill a small animal : 弋 .

DEER 鹿

Representing the deer 鹿 , with its head and horn 屮, its body ⼍ and its feet 比 .

DEFIANCE 艮

Defiance 艮 – a man ⼈ who turns around ⼔, to look (⊖ eye) another person full in the face.

DISH 皿

Picture of a dish mounted on a pedestal 皿, as used by the Chinese during banquets.

DISINTEGRATION 歹

Picture of a skeleton 歺 – the body after the decay of the flesh.

DIVINATION 卜

Cracks in tortoise shells 卜 , developed by heating, used as basis for fortune-telling.

* DOG 犬. 犭

A dog, showing its two front legs and its head turned aside 犬 .

DO NOT 毋

A woman 女, who is being locked up — for misconduct: 毋 .

* DOOR 門

Picture of a saloon-door with swinging leaves 門 .

DOORLEAF 戶

The left-hand leaf 戶 of a swinging-door 門.

DOT 丶

Picture of a dot • .

Rad5

DOWNSTROKE 亅

A crooked downstroke made by the writing-brush 丿.

DRAGON 龍

*A dragon flying towards the sky (dragon , wings , and the sky 二).**

DRUM 鼓

A drum (a hand 彐 holding a stick — beating a drum on a stand); a hand holding a stick (repeated): .

** DWELLING 宀

Picture of a hut - a primitive dwelling 八.

EAR 耳

Picture of the ear .

** EARTH 土 . 扌

The layer 二 from which all things 丨 came out: 土.

EARTHENWARE 缶

Picture of a vessel with a cover .

EIGHT 八

A quantity consisting of two equal halves) 八.

EMBROIDERY 黹

Cloth 巾 (a radical) pierced by thread and needle resulting in a piece of embroidery (a plant in full bloom): .

ENCLOSURE 囗

Picture of an enclosure 〇.

ENTER 入

Representing a plant with its roots penetrating the soil 人.

EVEN 齊

A field of corn, drawn in perspective, in which the ears are of even height 𠦳.

EVENING 夕

A wavy half-moon, just appearing above the horizon ☽.

** EYE 目. 罒

Picture of an eye ⟨⟩, set upright ⊖ in order to take up minimum space.

FACE 面

The face ◯ with the nose ⊜ in the center: ⊚.

FATHER 父

A hand ⟩ holding a rod | , to express authority: ⟩.

FIELD 田

Picture of a field with furrows ⊕.

FIGHT 鬥

Two pair of hands ⟨⟩ opposing each other: ⟨⟩.

** FIRE 火. 灬

A pile of wood burning with flames 火.

* FISH 魚

Picture of a fish: head 勹, scaly body ⊗, and tail 火 : 魚

*** FLESH 肉 . 月

Strips of dried meat, bundled together 肉.

FLUTE 龠

Representing a bamboo 龠 *tube with holes* ʊʊʊ: 龠.

FLY 飛

Picture of a flying crane 飛.

FOLDED HANDS 廾

Two hands joined together and held up in a respectable greeting, the way Chinese people do 廾.

* FOOD 食 . 食

A pot with contents ⊙, *a ladle* 匕, *and the symbol* 亼 *to suggest 'mixing' (three lines coming together):* 食

** FOOT 足 . 跙

The foot 止 , *with the ankle, heel and toes, at rest* ○: 足.

FOOTPRINT 釆

Representing the footprint of an animal 米.

* FOOTSTEP 彳

A step ノ *taken by the left foot* ㇄ *(* 仒 *the two legs of a person.):* 彳 .

FRAGRANT 香

The sweet 曰 *(a writing unit) odor of fermented (== vapors) grain* 禾 *(a wrriting unit):* 香.

GHOST 鬼

Picture of a ghost moving through the air 鬼 *(* 厸 *represents the swirl caused by the movement).*

Rad8

GO 行

Footsteps made by left and right feet: 彳亍 .

*** GOLD (METAL) 金

Four nuggets (ore) 𣎴 buried (𠆢 cover) in the earth 土 (Rad): 金 .

* GRAIN 禾

Representing a plant (木 Tree) with ripening ears hanging down 𠂆 at the top: 禾 .

*** GRASS 艸 . 艹

Representing grass, growing in abundance 艸 .

GREEN 青

The color (𠙻 crucible containing substance • colored by heat) of young plants 𡳥 emerging from the earth 土 (a Radical, see p. 34): 靑 .

GROW 生

A young plant 𡳥 emerging from the earth 土 (a Radical, see p. 34): 生 .

HAIR 毛

Picture of a bundle of hair 毛 .

HAIRLOCKS 髟

Representing long 镸 (Rad. 190) hairlocks 彡 : 髟

HALBERD 戈

Representing a halberd – a spear ending in a battle-axe: 戈 .

*** HAND (1) 手 . 扌

Picture of the hand with the five fingers clearly shown 手 .

Rad 9

HAND (2) 又.

The right hand seen in profile – only three fingers are seen: ∋

HEAD (1) 首

Representing the head with the hair clearly shown 𦣻.

* HEAD (2) 頁

The head 𦣻 *placed upon the body* 儿 : 頁

*** HEART 心. 忄

Picture of the heart – the sac opened; the lobes and the aorta are also seen ⺗.

HEMP 麻

Representing hemp (林 *plant) in storage* (广 *shelter):* 麻.

HIGH 高

Picture of a tower: 高

HORN 角

Representing a striated horn 角.

* HORSE 馬

Picture of a horse with its mane blowing in the wind: 馬.

ICE 冫

Picture of ice crystals 仌.

** ILLNESS 疒

To be ill and be lying ___ in bed 爿 *(splitwood: half of a tree* 木*):* 疒.

INCH 寸

A hand   *and a dash –, to indicate where the pulse can be felt – which is about an inch (Chin. inch < ca. .33 dm >) away from the hand:* ∄.

** INSECT 虫

Picture of a worm or insect ⌇.

INTERTWINE 爻

To unite by twisting together 爻.

** JADE 玉 . 王

The precious gem • that only kings 王 *(the mediator | between Heaven* ⊤ *, Earth* — *and Man* — *) could possess:* 玉.

** KNIFE 刀 刂

Picture of a knife 刀; *later the handle was curved upwards for compactness* 刀.

LAME 尢

Picture of a person who has one leg shorter than the other, and therefore has to limp 尢.

LANCE 矛

Picture of a lance 矛.

LEATHER 韋

Two men 刂刂 *stretching a piece of leather* ◯ *to smoothen it* 韋.

LEEK 韭

Picture of a leek plant 韭.

LEFTSTROKE ノ

A stroke written from right to left ノ – *general idea of action or motion.*

LEGS 儿

Representing the legs of a person 儿 .

LID 亠

Representing the lid of a vessel' 人 .

LINES 彡

Three lines – to represent rays of light, feathers, hair, etc. 彡 .

LITERATURE 文

Intercrossing lines, representing waves of thoughts 文 .

LONG 長

Hair 𠂉 so long that it is tied with a band—and a brooch 丫 : 𢄼 .

*** MAN 人 . 亻

That being who is standing on two legs 人 .

MELON 瓜

Picture of the melon plant and its fruit 瓜 .

MILLET 黍

Representing the plant 禾 , the seeds of which are put ∩ in water 巛 , to produce spirits: 黍

MINISTER 臣

Picture of a minister making a deep bow ⌓ before the Emperor. (The character was turned upright for compactnes 臣 .)

MOON 月

Picture of a crescent moon 月 .

MORTAR 臼

Representing a mortar ∪ with crushed material ∴ in it: 𐀃.

* MOUND 阜. 阝

Representing a terraced embankment ⌐ with steps ≡ leading to a forest (ooo trees): 𐀃

MOUNTAIN 山

Picture of a mountain range ⌒⌒.

*** MOUTH 口

Picture of the mouth ▽.

* MOVE ON 夂

Representing the long strides made by a person: 𐀃

NET 网. 罒. 网. 罓

Picture of a net (𐀃.

NOSE (1) 自

Picture of a nose 𐀃.

NOSE (2) 鼻

The nose 𐀃 on the human body (represented by 畀): 𐀃

NOT 兀. 尢

A man (represented by his two feet 儿) unable to stand up, beause of an obstacle 工: 𐀃.

OFFEND 辛

To offend (a pestle 𐀃 producing a grinding action) one's superior 二: 𐀃.

OLD 老. 耂

Hair Ψ and beard ∩ that have changed in color (a person ⟩ who has changed his position Ц – is upside down): 耂 .

ONE 一

One stroke, to represent the number 'one' : — .

OPPOSITION 舛

Two objects placed back to back ヺ屮 .

OX 牛. 牜

Representing an ox (seen from behind): only the two hind legs and tail are seen 十 ; the head is shown with the horns Ψ : 牛 .

PECK 斗

Ten 十 ladles 𝖯, which was a peck (measuring unit): 𝖯十 .

PERIOD 辰

A woman who bends over 𝖥 (cp. ∧ person) to conceal her menses (a sitting woman with apron 瓜): 辰 .

PERSEVERE 夂

A person 𝖭 who steps forward slowly despite shackles ﹨: 夂 .

PESTLE 干

Picture of a pestle 午 .

PIG 豕

Picture of a pig 豕 .

PIG'S SNOUT 彑. 彑. 彐

Representing a pig's snout 彑 .

PIT 凵

Representing a hole in the earth 凵 .

PLOW 耒

Representing a plow – the wooden (米 tree) handle and a piece of wood with dents in it 耒 : 耒 .

** PROCEED 辵 . 辶 . 辶

To proceed step by step (the foot 止 and 彳 three footsteps): 辵 .

PURSUE 夂

A man 人 who walks despite an obstacle ㇏ : 夂 .

RAIN 雨 . 霝

Drops of water = = falling down | from clouds ⌒ suspended from the sky ￣ : 雨 .

RAT 鼠

Picture of a rat, showing its head with whiskers ⿺, legs and tail 鼠 : 鼠 .

RAWHIDE 革

A pair of hands ⿰ stretching out a sheep's skin ⺜ : 革 .

REACH 至

A bird with wings backward ⿱ coming down and reaching the earth 土 : 至 .

RED 赤

Representing an angry man 大 – his face turning red (火 fire): 赤 .

* REVELATION 示 . 礻

Emanations 小 from heaven 二, revealing signs from heaven: 示 .

Rad15

RICE 米

Four grains of rice, scattered ✕ due to thrashing 十: 米.

RIVER 川 . 巛

A big stream formed by smaller streams 巛.

ROD 丨

A vertical stroke representing a rod 丨.

ROLL 疋

The foot 止 in motion ⊂: 疋.

RUN 走

A man with his head bent downward 夭 who runs (止 foot) quickly: 走.

SALT 鹵

A vessel ⊗ containing grains of salt ∵: 鹵.

SCHOLAR 士

*One who has knowledge of all things (between the two units one —
and 十: 士.*

SEAL 卩 . 已

*The right half of a broken seal 卩 given to a government official by
the Emperor (who held the left half 𠂤).*

SEE 見

The eye 目 of a person (a being standing on two legs 儿): 見.

SEIZE 隶

A hand 彐 that catches a running animal by its tail 㐌: 隶.

SELF 己

Representing the threads of the weft: two transversal = and one longitudinal | ; at the bottom is the shuttle ∟ : 㞷. (Etymology?)

SHEEP 羊. 善

Picture of a sheep seen from behind: the horns ￬, four feet and a tail ￦ : 羊.

** SHELL 貝

Picture of a 'cowrie' shell, used as money in ancient China 貝.

* SHELTER 广

A hut ⌂ which is half-finished that serves as a shelter: ￩.

*** SILK 糸. 糸

Small threads from cocoons 8 twisted (⼩ spindle) into a thicker one 糸.

SKIN 皮

The skin ? stripped off by a hand ⇒ holding a knife ⊃ : 皮.

SMALL 小

An object) ⎣ split | into two: 小.

SOUND 音

Showing the mouth ⊔, the tongue ￥ , the sound ─ produced in the mouth and the sound waves coming out from the mouth ⹀ : 音.

SPEAK 曰

A word ∟ spoken out by the mouth ⊔ : 曰.

SPLITWOOD (LEFT) 爿

The left half of a tree 木 : 丬.

SPLITWOOD (RIGHT) 片

The right half of a tree 朱 : 爿 .

SPOON 匕

Representing an ancient spoon: 不 .

SPROUT 屮

Picture of a new shoot of a plant , i.e. a sprout: Ψ .

SQUARE 方

Representing the square earth with the four regions at the corners: 卐 .

STAND 立

A man 大 *standing on the ground* 一 : 丄 .

** STONE 石

Showing a stone ○ *in a cliff* 厂 : 厈 .

STOOL 几

Picture of a stool 几 .

STOP 止

Representing the foot-at-rest, showing the heel ∟ *, the toe* ⌐ *and the ankle* Ϥ *of a foot:* 屮 .

STOPPER 両 . 西 . 西

Picture of a stopper ∪ *on a bottle* ⌐ : 襾 .

STRENGTH 力

Picture of a muscle in its sheath: 力 .

STRIKE 殳

The hand ∋ making a violent motion 仐 in order to strike: 殳.

STYLUS 聿

A hand ∋ holding a stylus | writing a line — on a tablet ⃞: 聿.

** SUN 日

Picture of the sun ⊙.

SWEET 甘

Something sweet — being held in the mouth 口: 甘.

TAP 攴. 夂

A hand holding a stick: 攴.

TEETH 齒

Representing teeth in the mouth : 齒. (凵 Serves as phonetic only.)

TEN 十

Symbol for a unit: 十.

THREAD 幺

Two cocoons ○ twisted into a thread: 幺.

TIGER 虍

Representing the stripes of the tiger: 虍.

TILE 瓦

Representing a Chinese rooftile ⃤, turned upright in order to take up minimum writing space: 瓦.

TONGUE 舌

The tongue Ψ shown outside the mouth ⊔: 呇.

TOOTH 牙

Representing a tooth: 彑.

TORTOISE 龜

Representing a tortoise, showing its body Ψ, its shell ⊗, and its claws
彡: 鼀.

TRACK 内

Representing the hind legs 冘 and the tail ㇄ of an animal – one that
just left its track: 扰.

*** TREE 木

Picture of a tree, showing the trunk |, with the branches ∪ and the
roots ∩: 朱.

TRIPOD 鼎

Picture of an ancient caldron with three legs, of which two only can
be seen: 鼎.

TURTLE 黽

Representing the turtle, showing its body Ψ and its gills ⊖⊖: 黽.

TWO 二

Two strokes, representing the number "two": =.

USE 用

Representing an ancient bronze vessel, to be used when making of-
fers to the ancestors: 用. (Etymology unknown.)

VALLEY 谷

A narrow opening (⊔ mouth) which is situated between two high
mountain walls 仌: 谷.

VAPOR 气

Representing vapors rising from the soil 气 .

VILLAGE 里

The fields of eight families 𦥑 surrounding a common well • , and the soil to be cultivated (土 earth, a Radical, see p. 34): 甲 .

*** WATER 水 . 氵 . 氺

A stream ⎸ with whirls of water 氺 : 氺 .

WHEAT 麥

A plant (米 tree) with ears of grain ∧∧, and 夊 (a man 𠂇) who advances in spite of an obstacle ＼ , indicating the relentless development of the grain): 麥 .

WHITE 白

The sun ⊙ just rising above the horizon, causing the sky to become "white": 白 .

WIND 風

Motion of air 𠘨 and an insect 虫. (It was believed that insects were born when the wind blew.): 風 .

* WINE JUG 酉

Picture of a wine jar 酉 .

WINE VESSEL 酋

A vessel filled with grain 酋 and a ladle 乀 to remove the wine: 酋 .

WINGS 羽

Picture of a pair of wings: 羽.

** WOMAN 女

Picture of a woman 女.

*** WORDS 言

The tongue 舌 *and words (=sound waves) being produced by it:* 言.

WORK 工

The ancient carpenter's square to symbolize 'work' : 工.

WRAP 勹

A man 人 *(a being standing on his legs* 人 *) who bends his legs to envelop a large object:* 勹.

YELLOW 黃

The fiery glow 光 *(a man* 人 *carrying a torch* 术 *) from the fields* 田 *:* 黃.

CHARACTER FINDER

CHARACTERS ARRANGED BY STROKE COUNT

Simple	**1** 一 172	**2** 二 173	七 178	八 179
	One	Two	Seven	Eight

九 180	十 181	力 86	人 212	刀 196	又 239	入 286
Nine	Ten	Strength	Person	Knife	Again	Enter

3 三 174	川 144	大 231	小 232	口 87	丸 1	工 57
Three	River	Big	Small	Mouth	Round	Work

千 183	万 184	土 146	上 117	下 118	子 213	女 214
Thousand	Ten thousand	Earth	Top	Bottom	Child	Woman

久 240	夕 241	山 145	**4** 手 89	毛 90	五 176	六 177
Long(time)	Evening	Mountain	Hand	Hair	Five	Six

双 187	少 186	牛 24	犬 25	戸 38	円 58	心 88
Both	Few	Ox	Dog	Door	Yen	Heart

王 218	氏 219	内 119	区 120	中 121	不 133	火 147
King	Mr.	Inside	Sector	Middle	Not	Fire

水 148	日 149	天 150	月 151 245	父 215	友 216	夫 217
Water	Sun. Day	Sky	Moon. Month	Father	Friend	Husband

A

242 分 Minute	243 今 Now	220 公 Public	277 木 Tree	233 太 Big	244 午 Noon	287 引 Pull
288 止 Stop	**5** 153 氷 Ice	2 甘 Sweet	122 北 North	278 本 Root	125 左 Left	50 白 White
188 半 Half	291 包 Wrap	246 冬 Winter	60 292 加 Add	234 巨 Huge	248 古 Old	279 瓜 Melon
267 出 Go out	221 母 Mother	91 目 Eye	92 皮 Skin	289 立 Stand	76 平 Even	222 民 People
197 皿 Dish	152 石 Stone	199 矢 Arrow	290 去 Leave	59 司 Manage	154 世 World	175 四 Four
103 市 Market	135 台 Platform	249 未 Not yet	124 外 Outside	134 田 Rice field	123 央 Center	189 号 Number
247 永 Lasting	198 玉 Jewel	126 右 Right	3 正 Correct			

Intermediate

6		
190	254	104
每	次	会
Every	Next	Meeting

294	223	136	4	182	127	185
回	自	字	安	百	地	多
Turn	Oneself	Character	Cheap	Hundred	Earth	Many

93	77	191	155	26	69	250
耳	吉	共	光	虫	米	年
Ear	Good fortune	Together	Light	Insect	Rice	Year

7	269	293	51	6	94	70
老	行	休	色	全	舌	肉
Aged	Go	Rest	Color	Complete(ly)	Tongue	Meat

128	253	27	5	200	268	251
西	先	羊	好	衣	至	早
West	Prior	Sheep	Good	Clothing	Arrive	Morning

280	224	252	270 7	61	298	95
竹	后	再	舟	売	見	足
Bamboo	Empress	Again	Boat	Sell	See	Foot

295	201	8	281	28	255	105
走	車	低	豆	貝	即	局
Run	Car	Low	Beans	Shell	Immediate(ly)	Office

君 228	赤 52	来 297	冷 9	良 10	男 227	卵 71
You. Mr.	Red	Come	Cool	Good	Man	Egg
利 62	私 226	身 96	寿 78	町 106	完 299	言 296
Profit	I	Body	Longevity	Town	Complete	Say
医 225	歩 8 300	直 11	空 137	東 129	杯 202	画 203
Doctor	Walk	Straight	Sky	East	Cup	Picture
表 206	宝 207	花 282	虎 29	到 271	店 39	房 40
Chart	Treasure	Flower	Tiger	Arrive at	Shop	Room
服 204	門 41	金 156	京 107	国 108	官 110	果 283
Dress	Door	Gold	Capital	Country	Government	Fruit
明 12	妻 229	林 284	青 53	受 302	所 109	物 205
Bright	Wife	Wood. Grove	Blue. Green	Receive	Place	Object
長 235	押 304	学 305	岩 157	夜 256	知 303	雨 158
Long	Push	Learn	Rock	Night	Know	Rain
河 159	取 301	海 9 161	春 257	看 306	計 208	皇 230
River	Take	Sea	Spring	Watch	Measure	Emperor

D

界 162	茶 72	亮 14	後 130	美 13	面 97	南 131
World	Tea	Clear	Behind	Beautiful	Face	South

前 132	秋 259	星 163	食 73	是 139	送 307	泉 160
Before	Autumn	Star	Food	Right. Just	Send	Spring. Fountain

若 15	室 43	飛 272	風 164	胃 98	香 138	屋 42
Young	Room	Fly	Wind	Stomach	Fragrance	Store

洋 165	昼 260	厚 236	昨 258 ⑩	竜 31	宮 44	骨 99
Ocean	Daytime	Thick	Yester-	Dragon	Palace	Bone

高 237	隻 192	島 166	紙 209	馬 30	時 261	書 308
High	Unit	Island	Paper	Horse	Time	Write

家 45	酒 74	旅 273	起 309	校 111	弱 16	席 210
Home	Liquor	Journey	Get up	School	Weak	Seat

夏 262	祥 79	特 141	航 274	真 140	値 63	
Summer	Good fortune	Special	Voyage	True	Price	

Complex 11

薬 285 Medicine	強 17 Strong	悪 18 Bad	黒 54 Black
船 275 Ship	華 112 Flower. China	黄 55 Yellow	第 193 Rank	都 113 Metropolis	鳥 34 Bird	閉 311 Close
鹿 35 Deer	週 263 Week	豚 33 Pig	商 64 Trade	雪 167 Snow	眼 100 Eye	郵 142 Mail
魚 32 Fish	問 310 Ask	堂 46 Hall 12	港 115 Harbor	貸 67 Lend	幾 194 How many	飲 313 Drink
短 238 Short	買 65 Buy	貿 66 Exchange	階 47 Story. Floor	開 312 Open (v)	筆 211 Writing brush	街 114 Street
朝 264 Morning	遊 276 Play	善 82 Good	飯 75 Rice	貴 19 Precious	場 116 Place	喜 81 Delight
晩 265 Evening	寒 20 Cold	湖 168 Lake	雲 169 Cloud	運 80 Luck 13	楽 83 Music	福 84 Good fortune
電 170 Electricity	業 68 Occupation	愛 85 Love	歳 266 Year old	禁 314 Porhibit	楼 48 Tall building	新 21 New

F

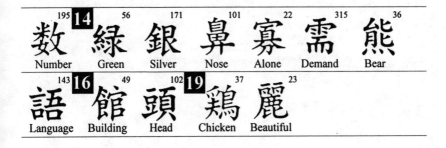

195	14 56	171	101	22	315	36
数	緑	銀	鼻	寡	需	熊
Number	Green	Silver	Nose	Alone	Demand	Bear

143	16 49	102	19 37	23
語	館	頭	鶏	麗
Language	Building	Head	Chicken	Beautiful

NOTES

NOTES

NOTES

NOTES

NOTES